T0381388

E.Q GYM

Become the Healer

April Wickstrom

BALBOA.PRESS

A DIVISION OF HAY HOUSE

Balboa Press books may be ordered through booksellers or by contacting:

Balboa Press
A Division of Hay House
1663 Liberty Drive
Bloomington, IN 47403
www.balboapress.com
844-682-1282

Because of the dynamic nature of the Internet, any web addresses or links contained in this book may have changed since publication and may no longer be valid. The views expressed in this work are solely those of the author and do not necessarily reflect the views of the publisher, and the publisher hereby disclaims any responsibility for them.

The author of this book does not dispense medical advice or prescribe the use of any technique as a form of treatment for physical, emotional, or medical problems without the advice of a physician, either directly or indirectly. The intent of the author is only to offer information of a general nature to help you in your quest for emotional and spiritual well-being. In the event you use any of the information in this book for yourself, which is your constitutional right, the author and the publisher assume no responsibility for your actions.

Any people depicted in stock imagery provided by Getty Images are models, and such images are being used for illustrative purposes only.
Certain stock imagery © Getty Images.

Print information available on the last page.

ISBN: 979-8-7652-5515-5 (sc)
ISBN: 979-8-7652-5514-8 (e)

Library of Congress Control Number: 2024918291

Balboa Press rev. date: 09/18/2024

This book is dedicated to all my teachers and clients. The exercises within are inspired by many influential pioneers, but the knowledge and development of myself and my clients have been crucial in refining these practices. Over the past ten years, I have held space for countless individuals on their journey to becoming their own true healers. This book encapsulates what I have learned during that time—what has truly worked for me and my clients. I have learned from each of you, and for that, I am deeply grateful. Thank you—you are all my teachers on this journey to love. A special thanks to Ninni-Henrietta Lundblad for so generously sharing her life story and wounds with me, and now, with the world.

INTRODUCTION

EQ GYM: Become the Healer

This book offers a self-discovery journey that goes beyond seeking quick fixes; it involves expanding our consciousness and embracing our emotions. Its aim is to guide you toward rediscovering the authentic version of yourself—the genuine unconditional love within.

Understanding self-development may be straightforward, but truly embodying that knowledge is a different story altogether. To bridge this gap, April Wickstrom, a professional leadership coach, and founder of the California-based retreat center The EQ Gym, has teamed up with Henrietta Ninni Lundblad. a former client. April combines Henrietta's relatable and sometimes humorous biography with insightful case studies and practical exercises to guide you to your own wounds, patterns, and suppressed emotions. This work is accessible and achievable for anyone, requiring minimal cost—just the price of this book and some of your time.

This book is divided into three parts:

Part 1: Life - The Story
Part 2: The Expansion
Part 3: The Practice

Part 1: Life - The Story

The first part presents a vulnerable story that will likely captivate your attention from start to finish. It encompasses elements of humor, occasional fear, moments of sadness, and complete relatability. Within these pages, you will meet Ninni, a woman who found herself trapped in her own thoughts, reliving painful events, and reopening old wounds repeatedly. She serves as a perfect example of how intelligence and being lost can coexist. Ninni's story will resonate with your own struggles of feeling powerless and trapped by life's circumstances.

Part 2: The Expansion

The second part dives deep into the realm of emotional intelligence. It delves into understanding our minds, defense mechanisms, survival strategies, and the ways in which our wounds manifest. This section requires your intellectual engagement and will provide you with a slower, more conscious reading experience.

Part 3: The Practice

The final part, dedicated to the EQ Gym, is all about you and the work involved. It centers on the transformative power of healing, a process that may span a lifetime—and perhaps it should. This section offers practices that can be applied to yourself and others, empowering you to become your own healer and potentially supporting others on their own journeys. It embodies the dance between your mind and body, a journey across the bridge in between. It entails building the most profound relationship you can ever have and necessitates self-love and dedication. This transformation emerges from practice, capturing the essence of April's proven healing modalities. This book serves as a self-healing guide, providing practical tools and techniques to help you become your own best healer. You will learn how to sit with your emotions and release negative beliefs.

The EQ Gym approach is centered on working with what is stored in both your mind and body. Throughout the book, you will discover medicine for the mind and medicine for the body. Over the past decade, April has guided thousands of clients worldwide to access their own medicine. Now, it is your turn.

Contents

PART 1
LIFE - THE STORY

1

GREAT. IT TURNS OUT I DON'T HAVE RECTAL CANCER AFTER ALL

Waking up to the sound of his guitar being strummed in the kitchen, I shuffle down the stairs to find him still in his pajamas, trying to perfect his morning rendition of "Wicked Game." I know there's something on his mind. I look at him, bleary-eyed and ask, "Do you love me?"

I know that he now will reassure me with his answer and the anxiety will go away.

Instead he looks at me with a forced smile and says, "Sometimes."

Sometimes? What does that even mean? Does he love me every other day? Is it when I've sorted his socks by color? When I wear his favorite dress? It's that moment, when reality becomes surreal and everything around me starts to lose form. And I know that nothing will ever be the same again.

We sit at the kitchen table, him with his guitar still in is lap and me with my mounting sadness, and he tries to explain the unexplainable.

I feel numb as he talks and my mind turns to all the things in our home that I will take with me when I leave . . . the porcelain plates on the shelf, the white blouse he always liked . . . And as I cry, I can't help but ask, "You've met someone else, haven't you?"

He hesitates, making me cry even harder.

"You have, I can see it in your eyes. Who is she?"

"No, there is no one else. This is about us. I'm not happy, and I don't think you are either. How could you be happy in this?"

"Oh, I'm just thrilled. I can finally cross rectal cancer off my list of things to worry about. Life can't possibly be that bad in just one week."

I've got a rectoscopy appointment on Wednesday. A doctor named

3

Philip Carter will be inserting some massive probe up my butt to check why I sometimes bleed when I go to the toilet. As an established hypochondriac, I've been counting down the months, weeks, and now finally the days to this date, which in an instant loses all its significance.

At first, Nathan seems relieved and probably thinks our separation will be smooth. Then there's a switch. It's so strange because now he's angry at me. He's yelling, accusing. We haven't had enough sex. I've been so mean. I've been so bitter. I've been so depressed. Poisoning our life with my health anxiety. We don't have fun together anymore. We've always been too different. The past five years have been tough, draining. At some point, we stopped laughing together.

Is he saying this or is it me?

Cliché after cliché is etched in me with small razor blades. Maybe it's not you, he says. Maybe it's just him. Maybe it's something else. Maybe he shouldn't have said anything until he was sure.

I cry. And cry. He talks. All his thoughts and contemplations spill out of him one after the other like sour burps.

The days after, I stumble around in my new surreal reality with my phone constantly glued to my wet, mascara-stained cheek. I smoke as many cigarettes as time allows and eat nothing. I can finally fit into those jeans that were always too tight.

Nathan and I are polite to each other. We pretend nothing happened, but everything is different. He's not the same. We don't talk in future tense; we only talk in present. He's not my husband anymore. He's someone I live in the same house with and who is thinking of leaving me. Who I know will leave me.

I'm swinging between dividing up our assets and figuring out how to deceive Nathan into staying with me.

I realize that I have been a difficult person to live with in recent years. I've been way too depressed, uninterested in sex, selfish in my thoughts about parenting, and fixated on my health. And where was Nathan in all of this? My entire life, I've been a person driven by anxiety, always on the hunt for what's wrong. As Nathan likes to say, "There's always a crisis that needs to be solved in your life."

When I got pregnant with Elise, it was like everything just calmed down. Nine months of living in the present, without much fear or concern about the future. Among our friends, we were some of the first to have a child, and we were completely oblivious to all the things that could go wrong. I didn't think about chromosomal abnormalities, heart defects, or premature birth. I was just present in my body, with Nathan. And he was with me. We were so young then, and never as in love as we were during those months. We were natural together, and the future was clear.

But when Elise finally came out—somewhat reluctantly after fifty-two hours of labor and the forced help of a suction cup—it felt like she came between me and Nathan. And all the intimacy that had been between us disappeared. Now there was Elise, constantly in need of closeness and presence. She had colic in the beginning, and every other night one of us would walk around and around the apartment with our screaming infant in a baby carrier on our chest and earmuffs over our ears. It was tough, but the misery was shared.

Six months later, she was the world's easiest baby—as long as we only followed her needs. The great thing about having a baby who screams intensely is that it becomes very difficult to ignore their needs. When she cried as soon as we put her down, we'd then carry her everywhere. When she'd wake up every hour if she slept in her own bed, we'd let her sleep between us. If she didn't want to sit still at the dinner table, then we'd follow her with a spoon and feed her in the middle of playing. The result when the colic disappeared was a confident baby ready to explore the world. But Nathan and I were left on opposite sides of our own needs. I had made it my life's goal to be the perfect parent in order to create the perfect individual: a happy person full of security and self-confidence.

When I was pregnant with Leo three years later, Nathan didn't want to take parental leave, and I said okay. Because I thought it was okay. But a few months into Leo's life, I regretted it. I wanted my own life too. I didn't know what I needed, other than a chance to be somewhere else, but Nathan refused. And that's when we fell apart. I became more and more bitter, mean, had anxiety attacks, and vented my pain with jabs, harsh words, and sudden and unexpected outbursts of anger that widened the gap between us with each attack. He's so conflict-averse and finds it hard to stand up for himself, so I just steamrolled over him.

Of course, he can't love me anymore.

I call my mom, not because I want to, but because I must.

"Oh, great," she sighs. "What did you do this time? Or is it someone else?"

"No, it's not someone else. At least, I don't think so."

My mom responds with silence, and I know exactly what she's thinking. Of course, it's someone else, because that's just how men are.

My parents got divorced when I was four years old. My dad had met Lena, a woman ten years younger than my mom. My mom's grief was all-consuming, cutting through us, our home, and her very being. She lost 15 kg. I remember the first time she talked about what had happened, we were in the car on our way to my grandma's. I was only seven years old, and my dad had moved in with Lena, into an apartment downtown. Lena, who sewed all her own clothes, wore blue eyeshadow, blue eyeliner, and had big hair that she put in rollers every morning. I liked her. My mom constantly asked if she was mean to me, but she never was. She was kind. We hung out together as a unit. My dad, Lena, and I rented movies, ate dinner in front of the TV, and played cards.

"You know, I never thought he would do it," my mom said in the car. "I knew all along that he could leave me. I knew he had others. But he loved you so much, I didn't think he could leave you. That's why it hurt so much when he did it. It was never for my sake that I was sad, only for yours."

Now I brace myself for my mom's emotions that come pouring over the phone line. Her initial certainty has now turned to worry. I'm worried, too, even scared, but my mom's concern for me takes over, and I quickly come up with a way to end the call.

Nathan doesn't want to get a divorce. He doesn't want to go to family therapy. He just wants to be left alone.

But I know we still have to do something, so I call all my friends and create my own form of therapy. It becomes my new hobby. I write long documents about why I love Nathan and how our future could be together.

"It's good for the relationship," explains my friend who did the same thing with a real therapist. She's divorced now.

I email my findings to Nathan and write there's absolutely no rush, but it would be good if he can do the same when he feels like it. He says he will because he knows he should. I write back that it feels good to write my feelings out and think about how I want our future to look, and that's when I realize how much I really love him. I write that I hope he will realize the same.

It's Wednesday and I finally have an appointment with Dr. Carter. I leave work at lunchtime and pass by the pharmacy where, on the doctor's orders, I purchase the biggest enema I have ever seen. It's about half a liter of water with a long pipette that is supposed to go inside me. I obediently fill my already empty stomach from the wrong end and wait.

After being cleaned out, my kindest neighbor, Jenny, drives me to the hospital. Jenny and I had only been neighbors for a few months when, a year later, I was admitted to the hospital for what everyone initially thought was a stroke. It turned out to be a panic attack. Nathan was home alone with Elise and Leo, who was only a few months old. Jenny offered to go to the hospital with my necessities and my computer, and Nathan, relatively panicked over the sudden responsibility of the children, gratefully accepted the offer.

I started crying as soon as Jenny came into the room. I'd always hated hospitals, and now I was stuck in some sort of medical technicality for what I already knew was a panic attack.

"Oh my god, we have to do something about this room," Jenny said, and resolutely rearranged the entire place. She pushed the bed, which stood alone in the middle, against a wall, climbed up on a chair, and took down the clock. Its ticking only amplified my already established panic. I fell in love with her then. She was fearless, motherly, and so resourceful.

Now, two years later, she is one of my closest friends, and she is always there when I need her. Today, she's waiting while I undergo the test.

Dr. Carter is a kind, slightly older man with glasses and white plastic gloves. I change into an apron with an open back and obediently lie on the plastic-covered table. On the wall hangs a small TV where I can see the inside of my gastrointestinal tract.

I talk unabashedly while he inserts the camera into my butt. I am relieved to note that I can barely feel it, probably because I already have such a pain in my heart, I think. "I'm getting a divorce, you know," I explained confidentially.

Dr. Carter smiles apologetically at me. He can't express much in this situation, which may be completely understandable as I lie on my side while his hand pushes the camera further and further up my butt.

I don't have rectal cancer. Dr. Carter explains that my intestinal is pink and nice. Surprisingly proud, I admire its ribbed, pork-cut walls that are displayed on the TV screen. Dr. Carter wonders if he should remove some hemorrhoids while he's at it. "It doesn't hurt that much," he says.

I can't sit in the car on the way home. Instead, I heave myself over the dashboard like a tragic version of when I was in labor. Jenny drives fast, and when I scream out my pain with clenched fists, she asks me anxiously if she should stop.

"Drive!" I roar and wolf down a Snickers between screams.

"But my god, does it hurt that much?" Jenny asks worriedly.

"I can't talk about it," I moan. "But it's worse than labor. And a thousand times worse than the examination itself. Jenny, you don't understand how much it hurts."

But she probably does because she stares grimly at the road and drives even faster.

Back home, I lie in the fetal position under a blanket and try to relax in front of my favorite episode of *Buffy the Vampire Slayer*. Josh Whedon is my household god and I've seen all the episodes a thousand times. Love, however, is quite problematic because only those who also love the series can understand how good it is. Most of them are also under eighteen years old. Nathan has never understood. He can understand that I love *The Wire* even if he doesn't want to watch it himself because the right people have told him it's good. But the reviewers, journalists, and private opinion makers who like Buffy are completely unknown to him, and most of them are women. That's why I almost always enjoy Buffy in solitude.

Now, however, it's hard to enjoy it because it feels like someone is repeatedly punching a fist up my butt. Nathan calls and asks how it went. When I tell him how much pain I'm in, he pauses, then says he's going to be home late. I think I've reached the maximum limit of humiliation now. But the next morning, Nathan goes to work without kissing me goodbye. I don't know which is worse.

2

FUCK BUDDIES AGAIN

A week later, I'm sitting across from my soon-to-be ex-husband, eating lunch at a diner near our jobs. I'm free from hemorrhoids, and he's free from emotions. We talk about nothing. It's not very pleasant.

"Do you like your job?" Nathan asks, because it's the only thing he can think to ask.

"I don't know," I say, because all I can think about is how he moved his foot in a different direction when my toe grazed his.

"You've been there quite a while now," he continues, building a perfect forkful of meat, sauce, and mashed potatoes. "Maybe it's time to look for something new?"

"Just because it's old doesn't mean it's bad." I'm lying because even though I'm so tired of my job, I'm also so angry at Nathan for thinking it's time to throw out everything that's old. Our relationship, my job—same, same. I listlessly poke at my shrimp salad and wonder what we're going to talk about. We talked this morning. And last night. And every day before that.

"Why haven't we done this more often? We work so close to each other."

"I usually have to work through lunch," Nathan remarks, looking around for the waitress. She's nowhere to be seen, and he fidgets as if his workplace will collapse if he's not back soon. "Lots of fires to put out at work today," he declares.

"Just like every day then," I say bitterly. Nathan hears it, but he pretends not to. He loves his job more than me. It's especially obvious now that he only loves me sometimes.

Next to us, a woman with a practically newborn baby in her arms is trying unsuccessfully to have a conversation with a man. Maybe he's her husband, but I hope not because he's so unaffected by the situation. Her baby just keeps screaming, and the lunch special in front of her remains untouched.

Nathan finds the waitress and scribbles an imitation of a signature in the air while exaggerating his lip movements to mime "Check, please."

I motion toward the couple next to us. "Another reason not to get divorced. Then you won't have to start over. What if you meet a young girl and have to do all of that once more?"

"Don't say that. Stop joking about divorce. You always say 'when' we get divorced. It'll become a self-fulfilling prophecy."

The waitress arrives too quickly, and lunch is over. As we leave, I take his hand. It's a gesture I've made so many times before, but now it feels out of place. I wonder if it's panic or stress about work that's making Nathan's gaze flicker like that. But I don't let go of his hand. And we walk together for a bit toward our respective jobs. I think that this is the beginning of change. That we're on our way to something else, something better. I'm glad he dared to say how he felt.

I'm on the phone with my friend Maya, wondering if my husband has possibly met someone else. Maya is one of my closest friends, and we talk every day. She's my go-to for crisis situations, always ready to cut through my biggest fears and fantasies with her dry, sharp insight. Maya and I share a mutual distrust of the world and the understanding that nothing anyone else does can ever truly surprise us. After all, humans are fairly simple creatures driven by clear needs.

It's Tuesday, and she's just picked up her kids from daycare. Between telling them to stop banging on the computer and making them sandwiches, she tries to give me good advice.

"It's just so strange that he could suddenly stop loving me from one day to the next," I say.

"But that's how it goes. You'll have your crisis for a year, and then everything will go back to normal. It's nothing out of the ordinary. He doesn't act like someone who's cheating. He's too grumpy and unhappy for that."

"Yeah, he's been so irritable these past few months. Gained weight.

Hasn't wanted to do anything. Hasn't even wanted to buy new clothes. Just wants to sit at home or be at work."

"Exactly. He hasn't met anyone. He's just depressed and needs time. You have to give him time," she says.

I think that if I can just make him realize how much I love him, everything will be okay. Maybe we need to take a romantic getaway together.

On Friday, Nathan comes home with a new coat from Paul Smith. It's great to see him taking an interest in his wardrobe again. And on Saturday morning, he runs his first mile. He seems to be feeling better now. It's probably because he's been able to get some things off his chest, I think. Now that he knows that I love him, he's been freed from that burden and is excited about life again. I pat myself on the back and compare us to other couples going through a crisis. Twenty days, and the crisis is over. Now everything can go back to normal. We just need to take better care of each other.

I decide to create a presentation with three travel options: a few days in New York, a weekend in Paris, or a longer getaway to Palma this summer. I decorate it with mood images and call his friend who lives in New York to discuss dates.

A few days later after we've both had a bit too much wine, I pull out my laptop and present him with the PowerPoint. We sit on the couch, and I lean my head hopefully against his shoulder. I feel a tingle throughout my body as I click through the slideshow. There is New York, with its leafy West Village streets and images of hamburgers and milkshakes. I've even pasted his friend's head onto a photo of someone in Times Square. And Palma, with white sun loungers and drinks by the pool, would do us good. The twinkling lights of Paris at night look so inviting.

But Nathan doesn't seem very enthusiastic at all. He sighs and moves slightly to the left, so that my cheek bounces off his shoulder and onto the couch. His lips are thin.

"This is really sweet of you, but I don't really want to travel anywhere with you right now. I need to find myself first, before I can make room for you. We've spent so much time together. Maybe too much. The last thing we need is probably more time together. Sorry. Are you upset?"

I feel like an idiot. Of course, he needs time. What was I thinking?

"No, it's okay. I understand. Maybe you can think about what you want to do and when. Maybe this summer then? That Palma trip? And Mom can take care of the kids, she's already promised."

Nathan doesn't answer, then says he's tired. So, we go to bed instead. My body feels heavy, now sober from disappointment, but Nathan is drunk and lies close to me. After years of deprived physical accessibility, Nathan has finally found the key to an active sex life with me: desperation. I'm so terrified, so frozen in panic about the possibility of him leaving me that I take every chance I get for validation. I try to ignore that the sex is rougher than ever and completely devoid of kisses. I've never wanted to kiss during sex before. Nathan, on the other hand, could go on indefinitely. Now he'd rather kiss my butt. And I let him. *Do whatever you want, as long as you're with me for a little while.*

These minutes before are the best ones. When he lies close to me and hugs me, as if it were perfectly natural, with his breath so close to my neck that it condenses on my skin. Now it's just like he really likes me for real and doesn't just want to put it in something warm, anything. But when we're done, he moves to the other side of the bed, with his head under the pillow.

I met Nathan when we were both too young, and he's younger than me. At first, we only slept with each other. Nathan told me stories about girls he used to be in love with, and I felt ashamed of sleeping with someone so young. However, he was cute, and when I was drunk, he kind of looked like Justin Timberlake. Eventually, I fell hard, but Nathan just wanted to keep it casual.

"Why can't we just have fun together and fool around?"

I cried and felt desperate when he said that, promising myself that we'd never see each other again. My friends said that he wasn't worth it and that I could do better. But when I got drunk again, there was never anyone better than Nathan. However, he still didn't want to commit, so I gave up on being in a relationship. Then Nathan thought he was in love, and after a while, I fell in love too. Looking back, I should have listened to him in the first place—he did warn me.

Every day, I religiously scroll through housing ads for two-bedroom apartments, switching back and forth between looking in our area and in the city center. Deep down, I know I belong in the heart of the city. I want to be strong, independent, and free in my very own apartment, decorated just the way I like it, without any compromises for Nathan's "bright and fresh" ideal.

I soak up images of deep-set windows and stately fireplaces and imagine life on my own. This is where my kids and I will live. They can share a room while they're still young. And this is my room, my very own sanctuary where I can sleep alone and binge-watch TV shows that only I love, wrapped in a big, cozy blanket that I don't have to share with anyone. And sometimes, the kids will snuggle up with me, and we'll watch a movie we all enjoy and sleep in a little longer the next morning. And I won't have a closet, just a clothes rack, with my shoes scattered here and there. Inside the kitchen, my wild, strong single friends from the media world—the ones I know so well through their blogs—will sit and laugh over takeout and way too much wine during the weeks when I don't have the kids. Everything in there is mine, all mine. Maybe I'll even get a cat.

Honestly, I've always thrived on being alone. It's Nathan who has trouble being by himself. He'll probably call me almost constantly, asking what I'm doing, wanting to hang out. But I'll be so caught up in my own life that I won't think about him except when he calls and when we switch custody. My life will be divided into the weeks with the kids and the weeks without them. And when they're with me, I won't be annoyed with them, I won't yell at them; I'll just be so incredibly happy that they're there. That their little bodies want to be in the exact same place as mine. We'll share the space when they're with me, and it'll be all mine when they're gone. And I'll be alone again.

Maybe I'll start my own magazine. It's always been a dream of mine—a unique way to approach the world of interior design. A personal and colorful publication that showcases interesting and unusual characters, people like me. The thought excites me, and I feel rebellious and energized. I forget all about Nathan. I forget that all I actually want is for us to live together, sharing daycare pickups and vacations—even teenage rebellions. I imagine Elise bringing home her first pimply boyfriend, and Nathan and I exchanging knowing glances and giggling secretly. And when Leo doesn't like his school and wants to switch, we'll sit with our teacups at the kitchen table, working together to find a solution, like families do. And then, when the kids move out, and we're in our upper-middle age, we'll move back into the city. We'll have time for dinners out, movies, theater, or just wandering aimlessly down the streets. That's when we'll be old together, feet touching on the couch, reading our separate books, and drinking wine in the middle of the day. I close my eyes and try to forget that I love Nathan more than anything right now and that he probably doesn't love me back. Oh, who cares about all that when I'm browsing homes, dreaming of my very own turn-of-the-century apartment with wooden floors and ornate moldings?

3

HE LOVES ME. TOO

My workplace seems to be going through some sort of crisis. Not entirely sure, but it seems pretty serious. It would be absolutely terrible to not only be a single mother of two, but also unemployed. But I can't take that in right now.

The theme of the magazine I work for is interior design, and I spend most of my days writing things like "Blue Autumn!" and "Sleek Lines." Today, I'm writing about a family who got tired of city life and moved to the country. Actually, it's not really "me," but more like my autopilot. Meanwhile, I'm thinking about Nathan and all the fun things we could do together, mixed with all the hurtful things he said that leave me feeling completely empty.

I leave my desk and go out to smoke two cigarettes in a row while crying on the phone to my sister. I figure that if I talk on the phone a lot during work hours, I won't have to risk telling my coworkers what's happened. Because I definitely don't want to talk about it with them. I can't help but burst into tears. Actually, I can hardly talk about anything without crying.

At the Monday meeting, we hear about an upcoming conference we'll all be attending. I'm guessing it's to discuss how to save the magazine from its inevitable demise. Somewhere in the middle of the meeting, I start crying. Not sobbing, just tears streaming down my face as if someone turned on a faucet inside my eyes. I'm torn between wiping them away and drawing attention to myself, or just letting them flow and hoping that people will think I got something in both eyes. I stare down at the table and soak my empty notepad.

"Are you okay?" asks Clara, our financial manager.

So, I laugh. "Yes and no. My husband is having a midlife crisis. Who knows, maybe I'll get lucky at the conference!"

I'm the only one laughing. Maybe the others find it hard to laugh when I'm crying at the same time. And it's not funny. But it seems to be the only consolation that people around me can offer. That if it ends, at least I'll get to experience falling in love again.

But I guess it'll be nice to get away for a bit, I think, turning enthusiastically to our CEO who's talking about Copenhagen's amazing cultural scene.

The conference is Thursday to Sunday. I don't want to go. I don't want to leave him alone without me for several days, missing the chance to fall in love with me again. I don't want to leave my kids. I don't want to be alone with my coworkers, without friends and the ability to cry every half hour. But I bravely chew my motion sickness gum, which conveniently makes me feel calm, and we all travel to Copenhagen.

At a conference, no one can hear you scream. Everyone is supposed to be friendly, happy, and super drunk. I'm drunk, too, but mostly sad. I cry when my boss shows graphs of the past year, I sniffle during brainstorming sessions about the magazine's future options, and I can't resist letting my tears fall on my pork-filled dumplings at the restaurant we had to book six weeks in advance to secure a table.

"He says he doesn't know what he wants!" I grip my editor's arm, hoping for some comfort.

She pats my hand and flashes a warm smile. "It'll all work out," she says. "All marriages go through rough patches. This is just one of those."

Maybe I should just leave him, I think. But then again, I'm not a quitter. I'll fight for this, even if it kills me.

"Think of the children," she adds.

Oh, right, the children. I'm thinking of them all the time—and Nathan. And after this weekend, my coworkers will be thinking about him too. I can't help it. I keep talking and talking, hoping for some words of wisdom from my colleagues. I want them to tell me it'll all be okay, to share stories of other couples who've been through the same thing and come out on top. And they do, but then they also share the ones who didn't. And of course, those are the ones that stick.

But on the last day of the conference, I managed to distract myself with some wine. After two glasses, life seems a bit better. After three, it's almost like things might work out. And after four, I can't even remember what the problem was. We love each other, we have two kids, a nice house, plenty of friends, and dinner parties every Friday. What's so hard about that?

So, I let my colleagues goad me into flirting with the young waiter. I'm sure he finds me irresistible, especially when I'm drunk. I drape my arm around him and ask for the best places to go in Copenhagen. He responds in Danish, and even though I have no idea what he's saying, I nod eagerly. I think he mentioned something about karaoke.

"Karaoke!" I shout triumphantly, raising my fist in the air. "Yes, karaoke!"

Two songs later—"Careless Whisper" and "Stairway to Heaven"—my colleagues gently led me away from the small stage in the karaoke bar I found on a side street near our hotel.

"Is it over now?" I ask. And I realize that yes, it's probably over now.

When Sunday arrives and we leave for home, I'm finally feeling happy again. But as the plane lands in a sun-drenched airport, the anxiety comes flooding back. Nathan and the kids pick me up, and we head home. It's so warm out, so we decide to grill. Nathan runs to the store, the kids play in the yard, and I sneak a peek at Nathan's phone. *Who's Leah?* Leah who he has coffee with every day at three. Leah who he eats lunch with on his birthday. Leah who he emails, wondering if she's emigrated since he hasn't seen her all morning. Who is Leah, and why does he say in an email that they shouldn't get so serious like last time, but that the only thing that matters is that they both are okay? My heart breaking into a million tiny pieces.

Leah is the reason why Nathan doesn't know if he loves me anymore. Leah is why he goes shopping now on Fridays to buy a new shirt, new pants, shoes, and socks in different colors. Leah is the one he thinks about every evening as he leans over his guitar and croons "Wicked Game." I leave my body and see it from above. I float up in the room until my back touches the ceiling and see myself standing there empty-handed with Nathan's phone in hand. I wonder what to do now. I run out into the garden and stumble into Leo who wants to show me his new elephant his dad has bought for him while I've been away. He holds it up in the air, so proud and happy and says, "Look Mommy, it has big, pink ears too."

I pat the big ears and wonder where I can take the children. Jenny and Danny are home, so I drop off the children there and rush up to the store. Nathan is at the checkout with a basketful of chicken, coriander, and mango, looking surprised as I rush in and pull him out of line. We stumble out onto the street, and I pant, shake, and say I did something stupid.

"I shouldn't have. I don't know why I did it, but I read your phone."

"You did what? What's wrong with you?"

"What's wrong with you? Who is Leah?"

Surprise, shock, anger, and relief fight for space in Nathan's face. We keep walking and end up in a park. We stop in the middle of the park, and Nathan looks at me. He sticks out his chin and says, definitely, "Yes, I have met someone that I . . . that I love."

What can I say to that? What should I say? I can't talk anymore because I have no saliva. I look at Nathan, who continues to talk about his new love. I see his mouth move, and he must also be low on saliva because small, sticky strands of it stick between his lips when they move. He says he loves me too. That he wishes I hadn't read their emails. That it's a completely separate situation that has nothing to do with us.

"But don't you understand that it means everything. How can we continue to save our marriage if you go to work every day and have lunch with Leah? What were you thinking?"

"You shouldn't have read the emails. You shouldn't have done that," he just repeats.

I stand up and start walking. He loves me. Too. I don't want to hear, don't want to see, don't want to be at all. My body hurts. Every part of it feels like a new part, and the world around feels like a new world.

Nathan walks quickly behind me. We follow along the small gravel path behind our houses, the one I fell for when we first looked at the house.

"Yes, but what do we do now?" he wonders. "We have to take care of this. We would probably have taken a break now if it weren't for the children," he says, showing how little he understands the situation.

"Everything is different now. I don't know if we can continue. We've taken a break, but now it's over. I don't know how to move forward. I don't want this anymore. I've turned myself inside out a thousand times to make you feel better while you bought new clothes for Leah's sake."

I don't feel any hope at all. I love Nathan, but he doesn't love me. He doesn't want to try. He wants to be with Leah. I don't want to be in a marriage with our children as an excuse.

We go inside, and I tell him I'm going taking the kids and going to Maya's. He says it's better if he goes. The omelet I had on the plane is trying to make its way up through my throat. I swallow and my stomach turns inside out, staring at the countertop as small white sparks divide into stripes. I drag my hands over it and bring everything on it down to the floor. I grab the big pewter tray we got as a housewarming gift from his parents and throw it on the floor right where he's standing.

"Get out! I want you to get out of here now!" I scream.

Nathan looks completely perplexed and scared for the first time. Nathan hates conflict, hates confrontation. I run up the stairs while yelling, "I don't understand how you could do this to us!"

Nathan leaves. He takes the car and drives away. I hope he never comes back. I hope he crashes and gets stuck between the car and the ground with the steering wheel jammed in his stomach as his insides ooze out like yogurt through a hole. I don't feel anything. I don't see or exist. Invisible, I go to Jenny's and explain what happened while hoping the kids won't hear, because they won't understand. They're playing so intensely with the fort they built. I hope they don't wonder why I'm crying.

We go back to our house. I lie down in bed between them and read *Findus Moves Out*. We always read it when Leo gets to decide.

"Hey, Elise," I ask her, as she's the oldest. "Do you wonder why I'm crying so much right now?"

Elise looks completely unfazed but a little pensive and looks up at the ceiling while putting her cold foot between mine.

"No," she says. "I think you're crying because you're sad. Sometimes people are sad. And I think right now you probably are."

"Yes, right now I'm sad."

4

AS IF IT NEVER HAPPENED

I grew up in Gothenburg, in a small suburb where I went to school. I remember feeling lost on the first day of preschool, not knowing where to go. Everyone around me seemed to know each other, but no one knew me, and no one was particularly interested in getting to know me either. I probably looked a bit angry as I usually do when I'm serious. And I was a serious child.

I stood serious and angry in a corner of the preschool's yard. It was winter, and I had my little white fur hat on. I stood there, sucking on one of the balls that hung from the end of the string when Victoria came up and looked down at me. "Shall we play?"

And we did. From that day on, we played. We played at her house and my house. I ran between my house and hers with my arms full of selected clothing items and makeup from my mom's wardrobe. Then we played teenagers. How we dreamed and longed to be teenagers. In the years leading up to that and all the years after, we have been friends. We were friends when Victoria got a fake ID and stumbled around all the city's streets and into bushes, walls, and guys, while I sat at home waiting for life that didn't really want to come. We were friends when she got her first boyfriend, and I didn't have one. We were friends when she hated school but still tried, and I went to a different school that I also hated and didn't try at all. We will always be friends, and the day after I fall apart, she takes the first train from Gothenburg and moves in with me.

She dresses the kids and feeds them. She dresses me and tries to get me to eat. She picks up Elise and Leo from preschool and teaches them how to garnish a pizza with pizzazz. She listens and dutifully smokes as many cigarettes as I do when the kids are asleep. She offers no solutions. She asks no questions. She just listens. And smokes. And washes the dishes.

I am incredibly tired. While my head is on fire, my body weighs three times more than it usually does. Nathan calls every day, and I hand the phone directly to the kids. Nathan emails, and I don't answer. I don't know what I want. Well, yes, I want Nathan to love me, but he probably doesn't. I know that now.

Everyone asks me what I want. If I love Nathan. As if it's wrong for me to love him. As if I should realize it and stop. But I can't stop. I realize it's wrong, and I'm ashamed that I do, but I can't stop. My feelings that I should know better won't disappear. They're trampled blades of grass. I'm a blade of grass that refuses to break. It doesn't mean I'm strong, it just means I bend so easily, so easily but without a breaking point.

My friend Bridget, who is also Nathan's friend, calls Nathan. She wonders what the hell is going on. Afterward, she summarizes that Nathan is in shock. Shocked about himself and his behavior. Shocked that he may want a divorce. Shocked that he doesn't know. He knows nothing. He sits at his sister's house, hiding, picking his belly button, and wondering if he wants to divorce me, who he has broken. And I'm waiting for him to call and say he loves me. That he wants to try. That we shouldn't give up. That we're worth more than this.

After three days, he does. When he calls, and I don't answer. He sends an SMS. When I don't respond to that, he sends an email. He seems to have caught a glimpse of some form of light. I start to hope and agree to take a walk if he agrees to us seeing a family counselor.

We meet in a local park. I'm cool behind my sunglasses with a double dose of motion sickness pills in me, and Nathan is very skinny. He forcibly hugs me. I'm a stripe without arms. He presses his nose against my shoulder and breathes in. As if he missed me. As if that other thing is something that has passed. He asks how I want to celebrate my birthday, which is in a week. He asks what we should do on the upcoming summer holiday. He asks if I want to celebrate it together with him. He wonders what I've told the kids. He says that for our sake, he wants to try again. For the kids' sake. For my sake. For his sake. We sit at a café, and Nathan buys a brie and salami baguette. I just drink coffee. He offers me his half of the baguette, as if nothing has happened.

5

HERE COME ALL THE FEELINGS AT ONCE

Nathan moves back home. After being apart for five days, we're living together again. I schedule an appointment with a therapist. She's a cognitive behavioral therapy (CBT), of course. I don't want to scare him away. CBT is therapy-light, therapy for those who don't really need therapy. Perhaps we don't need therapy. Perhaps we just need to move on and move apart. But this is the only way I know how to proceed.

So, we sit there in Phoebe's armchairs with two glasses of water between us. Like a triangle with Phoebe at the head. She draws a picture schema on her whiteboard.

Leave.

Stay and dwell.

Stay and move on.

These are our options. Nathan answers with a resounding yes to choosing number three. He doesn't want to dwell at all, he wants to move on. He was never in love with Leah, he explains now. She was just a fling at work, and he thinks I should delete the conversation we had about him being in love with her from history. He wants to invest in us now, he says. Not for the sake of the children. Not for the sake of security. But because we deserve it. Because we owe it to our life and the ten years we've had together. I drown in his words. Like a soft cotton bandage, they wrap around my bruised heart. I believe him because I want to believe him. Because I have no choice but to believe him.

I don't want to leave. I also realize that option number two is a rhetorical option, and the only thing I should answer in CBT is number three. So, I promise to move on. I promise not to dwell. Nathan gets a book on how to practice love: *The Act of Love* is the title and its third on our reading list. I get tips on a mindfulness app. The therapist explains to me that I have an abundance of emotions. That I must practice how to manage them, so they don't spray in all directions. Nathan agrees. He, in turn, will practice pretending to be in love. Because if you pretend long enough and hard enough, you eventually fall in love, explains the therapist.

Nathan seems to think that Phoebe is very wise. I know I must trust Phoebe because she's our last hope right now. She's going to save our life, our love, and our family, and if we just do as she says, everything will be fine. So, I stay and move on. Don't talk about Leah. Don't cry over Leah. Don't get angry about Leah. Don't think about Leah.

Home is peaceful now. We almost feel a little in love. Nathan spoons me when we go to sleep. He casually puts his hand on my leg when we have lunch with some friends. He kisses and hugs me when I get sad. I feel loved, and it's a drug too good to decline.

My friends are confused and seem to not believe that everything can be magically fixed overnight. They wonder where my anxiety has gone. Am I not sad? How can I be sad when I finally got what I wanted—a Nathan who loves me again. That's why I stay and keep moving forward. Right now, it feels true that I don't feel any sense of betrayal, jealousy, or bitterness. The euphoria of Nathan's rekindled love is so strong that it keeps all the other emotions my friends think I should have at bay.

On Sunday, we have dinner at his parents' place. We only see them, Patricia and Thomas, a few times a year, once around Christmas, once in the summer when we visit their country house, and a few birthdays. This time, we're visiting them at their penthouse apartment in the city. Their family dinners are always catered by staff. Nathan thinks it's delightful, while I become incredibly uncomfortable and behave inappropriately bourgeois. It's evident in the servers' slightly disdainful attitude. I nervously thank them in places when I shouldn't, ask for permission when I shouldn't, and run into the kitchen one too many times.

During dinner, various topics are discussed. I, who usually consider myself an eager and driven debater, always turn into a meek and stuttering creature in these situations. I don't know who she is, but I don't like her. And Nathan's total lack of interest and engagement in my predicament frustrates me every time. He mostly sits and giggles in a corner with his sister. He doesn't notice that I'm so ashamed of my job that I almost start crying when his father takes an interest in it by asking if I currently have one. He doesn't notice that his mother yells at me for being stupid when I can't specify why the Swedish church shouldn't have compulsory attendance for students in the church. And if he does notice, he pretends not to. If he does notice, he's probably ashamed, not that his family is quite uncivil and disinterested in his wife and children, but because he views me as inadequate and timid. Nathan is busy smoking, drinking cognac, and teasing his little sister, or discussing the importance of his career with his father.

Tonight, I don't say much. I don't have the energy to try to make them like me. It feels strange that they pretend like nothing happened, even though I know that Nathan stayed here for a few of the days we were apart. It feels more than strange that I know Nathan's dad shrugged his shoulders when Nathan told him what had happened and said that divorce isn't the worst thing that can happen to someone.

I find my refuge among the children in the TV room. I sink down in relief on the couch with Elise on one arm and Leo on the other. Then Lucas enters. He is married to Nathan's sister. He is very nice and just as bad at fitting in at these gatherings as I am. Lucas is a little drunk, I think. He sits down next to me and Leo on the couch and asks how I'm doing, how things are at home really.

"It's good now," I say. "It's been a bit chaotic for a while, but now it's better."

"How nice to hear," says Lucas. "Because you hear such strange things. Megan tells such strange things."

My breath stops for a moment inside and I brace myself for what's coming next. Lucas glances at Leo and whispers theatrically, "Is it true that Nathan has fooled around with a girl at work?"

I don't want to talk about this. Not here. Not with him. I don't want to explain, not put the words in my mouth. Not after spending an entire evening with Nathan's family in various humiliating forms and then being further dragged down by having to apologize for my husband's lack of judgment to his nosy brother-in-law.

"Yes, it's true. They had a relationship. But I don't think anything happened. It was probably more of a platonic form," I say.

"Oh, I see. But it was with a girl at work, right?"

"Yes."

"And he's still working there?"

"Yes."

"And what about her. She isn't quitting then?"

"No."

"But god, that must be horribly difficult."

"Yes," I say and get up. "But you have to move on. Choose whether to go or stay and move on. And I want to live with Nathan. So I stay and move on."

"Wow, you're so strong," he says.

But I don't feel strong at all. I feel like someone who has agreed to a truth against her will, an agreement and a definition of reality that doesn't match my reality. I haven't moved on. I love Nathan, but I hate what he's done. And every day, he goes back to work again. And I just have to pretend like nothing's wrong. Everything builds up inside me, and I become so incredibly angry. All those emotions that I find so hard to control become overwhelming, and I go into the living room and say too loudly to Nathan, who is sitting in an armchair and speaking softly with his father about something important, that I'm leaving now.

"The children and I are going home now," I say again, struggling to remove a hair that's stuck in my eyelashes while looking around for Leo and Elise, who don't want to leave and are playing hide-and-seek under the table in the dining room.

I start crying. I shout at the kids that we have to go. I shout at Nathan that I have had enough, that I'm leaving now. I'm done.

"Mind your tongue," Nathan mimes with an icy glare.

I know how inappropriate he thinks I am now. How socially awkward I am. But I can't help it. I have to get out of there. I'm breaking down.

Nathan has been drinking, so I drive. Leo and Elise scream for sandwiches and for the light to be turned on, and they want to watch a movie in the backseat, while I sob and let out everything that happened that evening, and then some. I don't know if I'm angry or sad, but I think it's both. I rant about his dad, tear down his mom, mock their home, the food we had, and the fact that they're all lawyers. *I hate all lawyers.*

"And how pathetic you are for loving all lawyers!" I continue to shout. "And Leah too!"

Leah, who is a lawyer.

Nathan listens in silence and says between his teeth that he understands how hard it must have been for me when Lucas, that clumsy bastard, had to interfere. But he doesn't touch me. He doesn't look at me. And when we go to bed that night, there's an arm's length between us.

After that, he's gone back into himself. Like a soap that slipped through my fingers. And I realize that I lost him, his love, and all his involvement by committing the greatest sin of CBT therapy by choosing option two: dwelling.

6

ALONE TOGETHER

I live with an empty shell of a human being. I can't bring myself to look him in the eyes because I know I'll see the contempt there. His lips, already thin, won't even try to smile. I try my best to make them smile by pretending everything is okay. By moving forward and not dwelling on the past. *See? I'm not dwelling!* I'm enthusiastically charging toward the future, ignoring history. It was just a fling, and I don't care anymore. I'm not angry, I promise. But it doesn't help. He's somewhere else. It's most obvious in the pictures I take of him and the kids. When time freezes and he stares into the phone's camera, I see the emptiness and coldness in his eyes. And he's so quiet. I nervously talk about anything and everything except the things that matter.

We borrow his dad's boat and go out on the water. It's windy. I hate boats and usually have to pretend that everything is fine and laugh with the kids as the waves crash over the side. But today I'm not pretending. I'm not scared of anything anymore except losing Nathan and the loneliness he can leave me in. I take the wheel and steer the boat, hoping Nathan will realize I'm the kind of person who takes charge of situations, my life, and myself, and that I'm not afraid and pathetic. *Do you love me now?* But Nathan looks at passing boats and buries his nose in Leo's salty, tousled hair. He doesn't look at me at all. We dock at a pier and jump ashore. We sit in the sun and eat chocolate and vanilla ice cream. This must be a happy moment, right? *Now we're happy—can't you see it? Do you love me now?*

We have the kids between us as soft, little shields. Leo's cold. Elise doesn't want to go to bed. Leo wants to swim, but also doesn't. Elise falls asleep on the couch between us with her head on Nathan's lap. Leo lies in front of Nathan and behind me like a small "s." Nathan, who never had much patience with the kids, suddenly has all the patience in the world. They get all the love that I don't. I wish I could let them have it.

There's a parent-teacher meeting that someone has to go to, and of course, it's me. I sit there and know that the kids will have to change schools if I move out. *Should I move out?* I make dinner for the kids and put them to bed, then we sit facing each other on the couch again. He's behind his computer, and I'm behind mine. Sometimes when he stretches out his legs, his foot comes to rest next to my thigh, and I think, "Now, surely it's over. Surely, he loves me again?" I don't touch his foot. I sit still. Oh, so still. Afraid to move in case he realizes he's touching me. Eventually, the stillness makes my leg cramp, and I move it slightly. Nathan moves his foot too.

After my parents' divorce, my mom and I stayed in the house with my dad as a frequent guest. We fought a lot. My mom is a person with strong emotions who constantly reacts to her surroundings. Because she is conflict-averse, she never said it directly but conveyed her dissatisfaction with unhappy facial expressions, small sounds, sighs, and groans. She is sensitive to loud noises. At that time, there were no soft-closing door hinges, so I learned to always slow down the door before it hit the hard wood. She is sensitive to smells. God, forbid I removed nail polish and didn't immediately throw away the cotton balls with the pungent acetone smell in the toilet. She was sensitive to my friends. If we laughed too loudly, it was expressed with clear disapproval from my mom, usually after they had gone home. Mom is sensitive to small spaces, too many people, others' dislike, messy rooms, the bathroom door not being properly closed, the kitchen door being closed, me coughing when we had gone to bed. It was a bit like living with a child. But I didn't understand that as a child. Instead, I tried to adapt as best I could to avoid disapproval. My mom's mood set the tone for everything. When I got a little older, the fights began. I remember that was when I really felt close to her. When I dared to scream and react. I threw things, screamed at her, called her various insulting names. And when I crossed the line—which was almost every argument—my mom left. I now know it was because she wanted to escape the argument, but at the time, I always thought she was leaving me, that it was me she was leaving behind. And I wandered around the house in a panic thinking she would never come back. And every argument was punished with days of silence. It was like I didn't exist. When I was younger, I never really understood why. I would crawl after her and beg her to at least just look at me. But she refused.

The silence paused as soon as we had visitors. Then it was like nothing had happened. Mom talked to me again. And I was so relieved that it was finally over. The ice was broken, and we were a normal family again. But as soon as the door closed behind the visitor, the silence returned. I eventually learned that if I delivered a credible enough apology for my behavior, if I cried and showed true remorse, she would forgive me. And it became warm and safe again. I think if I delivered the same type of apology to Nathan, he might forgive me. And everything would go back to normal. But I don't dare because I don't know what normal is between us anymore.

It's the weekend and we're headed over to Natalie and Mitch's for lunch. I'm lying in bed, hiding my head under the pillow. Nathan's in the bathroom, and I'm pretending to be asleep. I'm thinking about better times. Any time is better than this one. The one thing that has always comforted me is that no matter how terrible things have been, we've always had laughter. But now, it's impossible to laugh because I'm scared out of my mind.

Once, when Nathan and I had just started seeing each other, but weren't yet a couple—in that awkward stage between "definitely not interested" and "probably interested"—we went with our friends Sam, Glenda, and Katie to play the rather incomprehensible game of Frisbee golf in the woods. When Sam threw his Frisbee, the throw was accompanied by a genuine fart sound. Nathan laughed. I didn't understand. It wasn't Sam, it was Nathan.

"But how can you fart like that in front of me?" I asked.

"It's extra funny because it's in front of you," explained Sam.

And I thought it was absolutely hilarious. He had been saving his fart for the right moment, and just as Sam threw his Frisbee, it came out. I was so in love.

Fart jokes are really one of the best things. My dad taught me that. He used to sit in his office and talk to me on the phone while farting loudly. We both thought it was hilarious. I especially did, because my dad was completely impervious to the fact that all his colleagues could hear him.

He didn't care, because a fart is always a fart. And because he didn't care whether anyone could hear him or not.

So maybe I saw my dad in Nathan that day in the woods. Maybe I just saw the fart. But it became one of those things that we shared only with each other. Although it took a while. The first time I made a fart involuntarily, we were lying in a bed that was far too narrow in our second-hand apartment, and I was on the verge of falling asleep. I was happy and relaxed in every muscle. I instantly woke up when I heard the result of my muscle relaxation. I lay still for a long, long time, wondering if Nathan was awake. But he said nothing. Neither did I. He must be sleeping already, I thought, relieved.

The next day, I had sushi with our mutual friend George. George loved everything that was silly.

"I heard you had your first fart premiere yesterday," he said between bites of a nigiri, and laughed.

Nathan had heard. He hadn't said anything to me, but he had to George. After that day, the fart was loose, and all means were allowed.

It's amazing how humor changes with context. Now that I'm lying in bed crying to the sound of Nathan's upset stomach, his farts aren't the least bit entertaining.

At Natalie and Mitch's home, it's warm and Elton John is playing a little too loudly. Jenny and Danny, are also there, and their sugar-high kids are running up and down the stairs with Natalie and Mitch's kids, competing with the music for the highest volume. Elise and Leo become shy. Elise stands near, so near, and Leo just wants to be carried.

We're having lamb sausages and vegetable ragout for lunch. Natalie loves to cook, and it shows. Everyone eats a little too much and begins to complain about how full they are. I eat sparingly as usual, even though I love sausage.

Squeezed between two pairs of people who love each other, I note everything they do that we don't. How Natalie stands behind Mitch and hugs him while calling out that the food is ready. How Danny kisses Jenny without a second thought as they sit down. They joke about each other's bad morning moods and too-large piles of clothes, and Mitch tells a story about Natalie and how she had a bike accident without getting hurt, but it was really embarrassing. And funny. Nathan laughs and interjects his usual sharp comments as if everything is back to normal. He doesn't touch me, but at least he's talking to me now. He raises a glass with me just like with everyone else, and I think, maybe it's over now. Maybe he loves me again and everything is normal. But it's not. Because when I absentmindedly put my hand on his leg, he stiffens and looks at me with fear as if I'm going to tell him something terrible, and when Natalie asks what we're going to do this summer, we have no answer.

"I'll probably be at the country house a lot," Nathan says, meaning his parents' place. "I was thinking of building a treehouse for Elise."

He talks in singular. Of course.

7

WHILE THE WORLD MOVES ON

Every now and then, I wake up and am surprised to find that the rest of the world is still spinning. Despite my tears during Monday meetings and my constant stream of miserable anecdotes at three o'clock tea, my colleagues seem more concerned with the next issue and their own lives than whether my marriage will survive.

A new girl, Naomi, starts on Tuesday. I cling to her like gum on hot pavement. When everyone else is too busy to lunch with Naomi, I invite her to the local Indian restaurant that we go to almost every day. I pick at my chicken tikka and ask her how she's liking it so far.

"Well, it's good. Or I mean, it's hard to say on the first day, but everyone seems really nice." Naomi dips her naan bread in her masala sauce and smiles hesitantly.

"Yeah, everyone's really nice, especially in the beginning." I press my tongue against my palate, hoping my oversharing won't take over during my first conversation with Naomi.

Right now, I don't have the energy to feel anything about the others. But usually, I think they're a complete bunch of idiots. Our editor-in-chief is French and great at his job if he's allowed to do it by himself. And that doesn't work on a magazine that we're all supposed to make together. And the others just seem interested in going home. By five o'clock, the office is like a ghost town.

I gave up hope long ago of writing anything other than streamlined reports about provocatively happy people in upper middle-class homes. And right now, that's all I'm capable of. But the few times I come up for air, I get frustrated that nobody appreciates me and my talents, which I occasionally see as magnificent.

"What happens to them later then?"

"Well, nothing. You'll see. It's just a little chaotic sometimes. But if you just adapt and don't try to go your own way too much, everything will be great," I say cheerfully.

"Okay, I guess that doesn't sound too bad," mutters Naomi as she scrapes her plate clean.

My meal still fills my plate. I haven't regained my appetite. I hope Nathan doesn't see how much older I look when I get this thin. I hope he can start loving me again.

"I'm the kind of person who likes it when things are always moving and shaking in the workplace. I want something to happen every day, otherwise I get bored," she explains.

Naomi is also the kind of person who likes to describe herself to others. I really can't stand that. I understand that she's new here, and she wants to skip over this period where no one knows her and all her positive qualities, where she's just a mannequin of who she really is. I get it, but I hate it anyway.

"Well, you'll definitely enjoy it here with us," I say, trying to be friendly.

Naomi could potentially become my new work friend. Someone who gets to know me as the fun and happy person who's not at all "in crisis." I hate being "in crisis." That's all that defines me right now. This parenthesis period where the rest of my life is on hold.

"Should we go out for a drink after work?" I ask.

"I'd love to!" Naomi replies, a little too enthusiastically for comfort.

It could be fun to go out and socialize, maybe meet someone else, fall in love. My new man also has two kids, but he's already divorced and works in a creative field where he's in touch with his emotions. Not at all like Nathan, who's an economist and barely has any emotions. We'll move to the south side together. Nathan will be so devastated when it's me who wants a divorce. Then he'll realize how much he really loves me. But it won't matter anymore because I'll love someone else.

So, when the workday officially ends, we go to Oscar's where, as usual, there are way too many people. After a few too many glasses of wine at the bar, Naomi and I are pressed up against a wall in the aisle near the kitchen, trying to talk. We can't really hear each other, but it doesn't matter because we don't really have anything to say. I look around for someone to fall in love with. Preferably someone I already know, but anyone with feelings will do. But there are too many people, and I'm a little too drunk. They're pushing against me and up against the wall, and Naomi disappears into a conversation with someone else. I long for Nathan. The other Nathan, the one who loved me.

I hide in the bathroom. I don't want to go home, but I don't want to stay either. I cry away all my makeup while pushing through the heavy crowd of newly divorced media people and out onto the sidewalk to console myself with a cigarette. And there's Devon.

Devon was a love that never happened. He was too young, and I had just met Nathan. Plus, he was too unhappy and complicated. I'm usually unhappy, too, and I thought we'd have a pretty miserable life together. Now Devon isn't young anymore, he's in his thirties like me, and he's lost his hair. He's probably still unhappy. But he's still Devon, someone I've never really been able to forget. He's the one who stayed and settled inside of me so we could talk and continue to meet in dreams and all the transit stretches when I needed to rest my mind. Now he's standing in front of me for real, tilting his head and asking how I'm doing. I hug him a little too tightly, a little too long, while crying way too much. "Come on," he says, "let's go to Babs to talk for real."

I love Babs. Always have. The night Devon and I fell in love, we sat there for hours. It was one of those nights when you cover everything needed to realize how much you like each other. We talked about our parents, who we were in our teens, the music we loved, and the movies we hated. We talked about politics and all the times we had been at our unhappiest and a few times when we had been happy. Then I rode him home on my bike and that was it. And that was all it ever was. But we continued to have those conversations. Devon probably has them with everyone. And I've never forgotten him. Though, I was pretty sure he forgot about me.

But not now. Now he sits across from me at a small round table at our favorite spot and looks at me as if I'm the only one there. People are crowded around the bar and tables. Some eat, everyone drinks. And everything around me feels soft and friendly. Devon says he doesn't want to talk about anything other than me—we're just going to talk about me now.

"It's capitalism," he says when I'm finished with my miserable story about me and Nathan's decline.

Devon is the only one I know who gets away with saying things like that.

"Everyone thinks it'll get better just by replacing the old with something new."

"Maybe."

"What do you think will happen?" he wonders, saying what most people around me probably wonder, even me.

It's a real cliffhanger, our failed marriage. A bit like wondering how you're going to die. I don't know if I want to know how it's going to end. Maybe everyone knows how it's going to end except for me.

"I don't know. I don't know how I want it to end. I love Nathan," I say and feel ashamed.

"But what do you love? What's good about your life?"

Yeah, what's good about our life? How am I supposed to know that now when everything about our life is bad? How am I supposed to remember why I love Nathan when he's just cold, shut down, and uninterested? I just remember that I used to love him and that everything was fluid and pleasant then, when we at least laughed at the crap. I want to go back there. When maybe he loved me too.

"I don't know," I say, and my knee meets Devon's under the table. He doesn't move his leg. Finally, someone who sticks around.

Devon kisses me up against a lamppost on the way from Babs. I haven't kissed anyone other than Nathan in thirteen years, and it feels really strange. But good. Devon smells like a man, unlike Nathan who doesn't smell like anything. Finally, someone who wants to kiss my mouth and not just my ass. Finally, I am loved. The kiss is soft and deliberate and lasts a long time.

Nathan and I will get divorced, and I'll move in with Devon in one of those cute little houses in the village. The kids will love him, and the weeks when they stay with Nathan, Devon and I will eat out every night. On weekends, we'll stay in bed and read our own books or watch an entire season of *Game of Thrones*. Nathan hates *Game of Thrones*. Devon will teach Elise how to read and Leo how to play guitar. Devon is very musical. Nathan will move in with his lawyer lady, and we'll only see each other briefly when we exchange the kids. He'll become someone who doesn't matter anymore.

"We're going to my place," Devon says.

"No, I can't. That would be the end for me and Nathan," I say and want to go home.

"It doesn't matter tonight. Nothing matters tonight," Devon says, overly melodramatic as he clumsily grasps my breast.

"But it does matter. I'm married, and you're thirty-one," I say, lifting his hand with my thumb and forefinger.

Devon tilts his head. Why does he keep doing that? Does he have water in his ear? He gives me a hug. Smelling like a man is smelling like way too much.

I take a taxi home where Nathan is sleeping with his head under the pillow and his arm over it. He doesn't snore. He never snores. I lie as close as I dare without waking him. I bury my nose in his scentless armpit and pretend everything is normal.

8

I LOVED YOU GUYS, YOU KNOW. I LOVED YOU SO MUCH

Three of my best friends still live in Gothenburg. One of them is Victoria and the other two are Bridget and Rachel. Every year, we go to Rachel's husband's hotel in the south. It's right by the sea and feels like home. In the summers, I go there with Nathan and the kids, and Rachel, Bridget, and Victoria with their families. But twice a year, once in the fall and once in the spring, we go just the four of us. We go to be massaged in the spa (not me, though, I hate spas), eat, drink, and talk. Since the three of them live in Gothenburg, these weekends often turn into long therapy sessions for one of us. Usually, someone's life is in crisis, and we do our best to give advice or just listen. This time, I know it's going to be me.

I both want to go and don't want to go. I know I'm going to cry. I can't handle any more crying, but there's not much else I can do. I cry in the airport shop. I buy the perfume that smells way too flowery but that I know Nathan likes. I like perfumes that smell musky. I had this perfume the summer we got married. That summer when we should have been the happiest, but we probably weren't. We were already tired of the wedding before it even happened. We worked like animals with Elise in a carrier on our backs, clearing, painting, furnishing, throwing away, and renovating Nathan's parents' summer house. Everyone said it was a fantastic party. I barely remember it, but I don't think I thought it was fantastic then.

Now, I wish I were there instead of here, crying in an airport with just the perfume. I wish I could start over and not have been so angry and bitter and so incredibly worried and scared about everything that corroded Nathan's feelings for me. I now know that I ruined everything. I ate away at everything that was us with bitterness, fear, and anxiety. Every day was a new day when one of us could die or get sick or fall at daycare and get brain damage. Elise had too many bruises on her leg—it must be leukemia. I started every morning with a headache—it must be a brain tumor. That's what I read online, that the headache you have when you wake up in the morning is the worst kind, the one that's most likely something dangerous. When I got pregnant with Leo, I was sure I would have a miscarriage. And when I didn't and my belly grew and it was soon time for delivery, I knew that the delivery would be a difficult one with the result of brain damage. But Leo came, and he seemed completely healthy. Maybe with a small risk of Down's syndrome? I found pictures of children with Down's on the internet that I compared to pictures of Leo and eventually became quite sure that he had it. I Googled "how late can Down's be detected" and got lots of hits from parents who had discovered it as late as daycare age. But then the thoughts faded, and something new took over. Every night was a night when Leo could die. I had a breathing monitor that beeped every fifteen minutes, because it was probably broken, but it was just as likely that Leo stopped breathing. And I was glued to parent forums with threads about other parents who had been affected and who recounted their stories about angel children. But Leo didn't die, he grew older. However, he had difficulty speaking. He couldn't say "mamma" or "lamp," or anything. So, I realized that he was most likely autistic. I searched for parent forums and read countless pages about autism and found more and more signs that it was true. As a parent, you just know these things. They had all known it, and now I did too.

I don't remember Nathan from that time. I don't remember if he believed me, if he listened, if he got angry or scared. I just remember thinking that he worked way too much. And that I felt alone. Alone and responsible for our children's survival. And for my own, that if I died, they would be left with a father who worked too much to discover that they had leukemia and were being bullied at school. So, I ruined it. I cut our relationship apart with worry about things that could happen but never did.

The plane takes off, and I cry my way through the bumpy ride, completely unaffected by the turbulence. I was afraid of flying, but not now. I cry while waiting for my suitcase. I sit in the taxi with Maya's voice on the phone in my ear and look out over the flat fields rushing by on the outside and cry. Reality is so clear now that I'm not in the middle of it. Once I arrive at the hotel, the crying stops. I check in and drag my bag over the carpeted floors to the room that I'll be sharing with Victoria. And they're all there in the room. Victoria is smoking on the balcony, and Rachel is cradling her big belly in her hands (she has a child in there), while Bridget flips through music on her phone.

"Hello," I say and start crying.

Bridget reaches out her arms, and I take two steps into a hug. I cry a big, wet spot on her shoulder. I can't stop shaking either. Bridget says, "I know."

Rachel comes over, and her round, hard belly presses against my back as she hugs me too. Victoria gives up her freshly lit cigarette and envelops all three of us in a cloud of smoke when she joins our group hug. Shaking, I stand in the middle of the hug and can't stop crying even though I realize now that I should.

Bridget says I must decide what I want. She's been divorced for a year now. She's happy with a new man who loves her and treats her well. As she deserves. It took her a long time to break free. Maybe that's how it has to be, so you don't regret it. But then you regret it anyway. Since her divorce, Bridget is good at knowing what everyone else should do. I trust her; she's one of my wisest friends.

Rachel, always so principled, assures me that everything will be fine. If only I could have her pride and self-respect. She never backs down. And Victoria, always the fierce one, tells me that he can go to hell. She sees the world in black and white, which makes things easier. She demands respect and gets it. Maybe it's because I can't demand anything that I don't get anything. But how can I demand anything from someone who may want to leave me? I can only wait. So, I talk about Leah, the silence, and the loneliness that prevails at home now. About Nathan, who is there but not really there. And I can see that they don't quite understand how he can be like this and how I can accept it. Why don't I say anything? Why don't I demand anything?

They don't understand because they don't know what it's like when the bond between two people starts to evaporate and the familiarity disappears. When you're no longer allowed to be yourself. When I'm no longer okay. There are no demands I can make because he doesn't love me. How can

I demand that he be kind when he doesn't love me? How can I ask for tenderness and respect when he doesn't love me? What right do I have to be jealous of someone who doesn't belong to me? So, if I want to stay, I have to accept it. Of course, I have a choice—I can leave. But I don't want to. So, I stay and accept what I can't change.

"But what about you? What do you want?" Bridget asks while we're sitting in a giant bubbling hot tub on the roof, sipping champagne.

"I want to live in peace and quiet with my husband and my children."

"Do you love Nathan?"

"Yes."

Those words ring false. I always feel like a liar when I say them. *How can I love him when he's like this?* I shouldn't.

"You know, I think Nathan is panicking because he realizes how much power he has right now. This is new in your relationship; he's not used to everything revolving around him like this. You must take back control," Bridget says.

"You have to demand your right to respect," Rachel adds.

"He has to quit that job," Victoria says. "Or she has to quit."

I give up on my explanations. I don't have the energy to explain why he can't quit or why Nathan, who is his ex-mistress's boss, can't ask her to quit. I lower my ears into the bubbly water and wrap myself in their care and the annoying hum of the hot tub. I know it can be good again. Just as long as he comes back to the Nathan I used to know.

In the beginning, the first few years, we were the ones making out everywhere. And I always wanted sex. Sometimes Nathan was too tired. Can you ever be too tired for love, I wondered. The first time I said "I love you," we were in separate beds, he in Stockholm and me in Gothenburg. He fell asleep with the phone against his cheek, and I whispered "I love you" into the phone. He didn't answer because he was asleep.

His first time saying it to me was when I caught him in a lie. He had received a text message in the middle of the night that I had read. It was from his ex, asking if he was out.

"Who was texting you yesterday?" I asked when we woke up.

"It was Peter, asking if I had bought wine for Saturday."

It wasn't that he lied, it definitely wasn't that he received a text message that made me so sad. It was that he lied so well. Because Nathan was a nice guy, one of the good ones. He was the unexpected choice of partner that I was so proud of. A walking bundle of kindness that I didn't really deserve. Sometimes I was afraid he would die young because he was the type of character who was taken from the world prematurely. The young, optimistic, slightly too good-hearted man who had never done anything wrong. The one whose mother called him her prince and who still ended phone calls with his dad by saying "kisses."

He was also the one who stood in the kitchen and lied to me as if it were the easiest, most natural thing in the world. The one who was a little too thin with thin shoulders and the world's softest neck. I told him I had read his text message and he got angry, but above all he became remorseful. And then he hugged me and whispered that he loved me. It was a big moment. One that never returned.

But we didn't need words. We were so solid for so long. We were two best friends living together and loving each other. One summer, I was in Gothenburg, and he was still in Stockholm working. Once when I was there visiting, we fell asleep without having sex. And it felt completely okay. After that, it was almost always okay not to have sex. In the last few years, I just wanted a hug but was afraid to give him one because he almost always thought it meant I wanted sex.

And now I'm lying in a hot tub surrounded by those who love me, and I don't know what I want, but I know what I should do. I know what all my friends, monthly magazines, and romantic comedies say I should do. I should leave this man who doesn't seem to feel remorse, who doesn't show desire or willingness to change or compensate for his infidelity. I should live with someone who loves me for who I am. I shouldn't want to stay in something that's bad for me. I should seek something better. Or should I want to stay and fight because I love him, because we have two children together, because he says he wants it to be good. I don't know, it changes depending on who I talk to, what movie I watch, what blog post or book I read. I'm like a sponge soaking up all the opinions that come my way.

In this stage of panic and sorrow, I find it so hard to feel what my true feelings are. Logic and pride and all the world's literature tell me that I should leave him. That I'm just afraid of loneliness and that he will never love me again (did he ever?) and that I should bake some kind of pie that I can throw in his face and then walk away with the children into the sunset.

That scene feels good. My heart jumps triumphantly at the thought, and it feels like I can breathe again. The person who leaves, I am proud of her. She takes command of the situation, and she knows what she wants. The one who is me now and who stays is like toilet paper that the wind blows wherever it wants. It feels like all the friends and family and colleagues around me (and Nathan too) are waiting for me to see the truth and just leave. What idiot stays? What idiot stays in the cold and tries to create warmth with a sparkler?

Back home again. Nathan had a good weekend with the kids, he says. It's been much calmer than usual. Maybe because he was alone, or maybe because I was away.

"I want a divorce," I say, bursting into tears.

"Really?" Nathan says, looking cautiously surprised.

"Yes, I can't do this anymore. Enough is enough. I can't stay in this any longer."

A calm takes over. My body feels steady on the couch, and my breathing comes easily. The kids are asleep upstairs. Tomorrow, Elise turns five.

Nathan hesitates. He pulls on a thread on his striped shirt. "Oh, but I don't know if that's right," he says, as if the choice is his to make.

"We have to do something; this can't go on any longer. I can't stay in this," I say again.

After a while, Nathan seems somewhat relieved. We talk about whether I should stay, and if he can ask his parents for money for a condo. I think about what everyone else will think. We're the couple who plays fart games and who, during a dinner with friends, pulls out all our underwear in a competition to show who has the ugliest. We're the ones who are easygoing and fun, and who don't take ourselves too seriously. Maybe we should have taken ourselves more seriously. Maybe we shouldn't have joked about anniversaries, wedding rings, divorce, and infidelity. Maybe we should have taken care of each other more.

"How surprised everyone will be now. We were the relationship that everyone thought would last," I say, smiling. "That couple everyone loves to love."

Nathan starts to cry. Unfamiliar tears come out of him, like convulsions. He hides his face in his hands, and I comfort him, telling him that I know, but we'll always be friends.

"You're right, we're just too different. We like different things, we want to go to different places," I say.

Nathan waves his hand dismissively, "I don't think we're that different at all."

This is the second time I've ever seen Nathan cry. The first time was six years ago when we had our first crisis. We didn't have kids then and lived in an apartment in the trendy part of town. It was May, and we had finished renovating, painting, shopping, and decorating. We both had jobs that we were only half-satisfied with, and we were almost always annoyed with each other. The joking, almost harsh banter that was our trademark was no longer so funny, just hard. And I was very much in love with someone else. Nevertheless, frustrated with our relationship and the indifference that Nathan emitted, I lay half-dazed on the couch and finished a rant to Nathan with: "Sometimes I wonder if you even love me anymore!"

He walked into the room from the kitchen and looked at me. "Maybe I don't."

Felled by this completely unthinkable possibility, I burst into tears. "What? Why not? Do you want to break up? What do you mean?"

"I just think we're so irritated with each other all the time. It doesn't feel good anymore."

And then we talked. About what we wanted. How we could fix it. If we wanted to fix it. Would we spend the summer apart or together? And Nathan cried and I cried. We were terrified. But in July, we went to Greece. I continued to be in love with someone else, but also in love with Nathan. We didn't talk about why we ended up where we did. I didn't think about it much either. But we had fun together.

I realized that I loved him. And he loved me. When I went to tell the other guy, he didn't want to meet up. And I gave up on him. By the fall, I no longer remembered the feeling of the other guy, and all that remained was the anxiety that maybe Nathan didn't love me. In October, I became pregnant. And we were so happy. Wrapped up in a warm bubble of togetherness and certainty, we were actually happy. I gained 26 kg. and Nathan rejoiced in how it affected my breasts. We retreated into our happy little bubble, just the two of us. We ate the world's longest breakfasts accompanied by the morning radio. We bought ice cream and strawberries that we ate in bed while watching the entire second season of *Lost*. And I was so big that I could barely get out of it. But it didn't matter. Because we could stay in bed as long as we wanted.

Then Elise came, and after two weeks, she got colic. When she was seven months old, I had my first panic attack in ten years, and it just went downhill from there. When I became pregnant again three years later, I don't think Nathan really wanted any more children. He wanted Elise to have a sibling, but I don't think he actually wanted any more himself. I, who only wanted one child from the start, panicked when number two didn't happen no matter how hard we tried.

And now, my soon-to-be ex-husband is sitting on the couch, unable to stop crying. My fuck buddy, my roommate, my unhappy love, my fart joking best friend, my husband. It actually feels completely okay. Whatever happens, it will be okay. When I move into my artsy apartment, Nathan will be the one helping me put up shelves. And when Saturday comes and we feel lonely, we'll still meet up with the whole family. We'll love each other as friends. That was always what we did best.

"You're so calm," says Nathan.

"Yeah, but you have to understand. I've been prepared for this the whole time. I jumped to divorce already in the spring. I've been living with the thought of divorce ever since."

Nathan cries even harder. "I think I have too."

We end the day by wrapping Elise's birthday presents. I cut pieces of tape and Nathan curls ribbons and cries. Exhausted, we go upstairs and brush our teeth, and Nathan cries. We hug with toothpaste-foaming mouths. We lie down in bed, and Nathan wants to hold me. But there's my limit—it hurts too much.

9

IS THIS THE END?

This is something new. To wake up and not wonder. To wake up and know that it will happen, that the end begins, but so does something new. The end of living in anticipation of something I can't have and the beginning of living in the safe knowledge of what I have: myself and my children. I free myself from Leo's tight grip, glance at Nathan who sleeps on his back with his mouth open and tear-swollen face. I don't want him to wake up. I want to be alone now that I'm going to be alone.

I drink coffee in the kitchen and gaze over our open floor plan. I see all the books that are his in the bookcase. He probably doesn't even want them. Most of them were given to him by his mother anyway. The TV that stands on a cart he built. He probably doesn't want that either. He's always complained about the TV, that it's too big, and do we even need a TV? He might like that modular candleholder made of tin. I bought a few of them on auction, actually he bought some too. But then . . . there's nothing. Nothing that he will want to take with him. Well, maybe that painting. The one about a shattered relationship, he's always liked that. The rest is mine.

10

THE REAL DIVORCE

The first time I met Erik, he and his wife, Hazel, were having a party in the common area of our terraced houses. They were new, young, and beautiful, and served Coke with personalized labels. Nathan and our neighbor besties stood in a group, snickering loudly at the event. We tried to come up with a conversation about the speed signs on our street, and Erik giggled and squinted at us, saying, "But don't we all like to speed up the street a bit?"

I don't know if he was joking, but he seemed pretty dumb. Plus, he was short, had close-set eyes, and was wearing pink shorts, a white Ralph Lauren shirt, and brown suede Prada loafers. Everything I despise in a little ginger meatball.

Nathan and I never actually got divorced. The night we decided to separate was a turning point. Nathan started crying. And feel. After that we fought for our relationship for three years. We clung to each other desperately and stubbornly, while the wall between us grew higher. Nathan continued to have second thoughts a few times, about every three months or so. The imbalance between us was constant. I desperately tried to become myself again. But I sensed his every breath, every minute, every second. Finally, we moved apart. On a trial basis. I started taking antidepressants and felt that it was perfectly okay to live alone or with Nathan. And somehow, we found our way back. After six months, we moved back in together. A year later, Nathan's company made a lot of money, so we sold our terraced house to an old friend of Nathan's, and moved to bigger house a few blocks away. A much bigger house. Nathan and I were doing pretty well. At least, I thought we were. He thought so too. We went back to scheduled sex once a week, and I decorated our new house with pastels and modern furniture mixed with old favorites. A magazine even did a home tour of our house. I appeared spontaneous and delightful with lots of self-awareness. Life felt good again. But we still never talked about love. We became a bigger and bigger family in our new neighborhood. We practically merged with, Jenny and Danny, their two sons, and Natalie and Mitch, and their children. Together, we traveled, celebrated Christmas, New Year's, Easter, practically every weekend and many weekdays together. Life was mild and embracing. Of course, I got restless. Quit my job. Started doing yoga. Started a company with Jenny to become interior designers. Went to a psychiatrist and got antidepressants, went to an osteopath, went to an aesthetician, tried psychoanalytic therapy, Gestalt therapy, CBT therapy. Got an ADHD diagnosis. Then we met Hazel and Erik, and life did a summersault. For real this time.

The next time we meet is at Nathan's buddies from Gothenburg, Ben and Sheila's place. I come directly from a full-day coaching course to our old house where Ben and Sheila now live with their two kids. Ben is besties with Erik and wants the four of us to become close too. I'm skeptical, but since everyone describes him as funny, I decide to give him a chance. It's a French-themed dinner, and I wear a blue, white, and red knit sweater that's way too tight. I'm seated next to Erik, drink too much wine, and discuss politics. I realize that Erik has been prepped by Ben to profile me and comes prepared with arguments. He's very right-wing, and of course, I become extra left-wing to maximize the discussion. It goes well until I run out of arguments, and Erik runs out of manners. After a while, he and Ben go outside to smoke weed, and we don't talk much more. I don't think I like Erik. He's self-righteous and completely uninterested in anyone else's arguments but his own.

But everything changes with a joke. It's the day after Nathan's fortieth birthday party, and Jenny and I go to Erik and Hazel's to pick up my and Nathan's car that Erik borrowed from the party venue the day before. He and Hazel had to leave the party in a panic after the babysitter called to say their daughter had fallen and hit her head. It had left me without a table partner because Erik was supposed to sit next to me. I had placed him there for lack of anyone else. I didn't know who else would endure sitting next to him because he loves to provoke anyone who comes near him.

When Jenny and I arrive in the garage driveway, Erik is clearing junk from the garage. Hazel is having a birthday party in a few days; she's turning thirty-four. He looks up happily when he sees us. He's entirely unattractive to me. Short, stocky, and a bit old man-like in his appearance. He's wearing a pair of light shorts and a white tennis shirt. His reddish hair stands in stiff spikes on top of his head, and he's warm and a little sweaty on his upper lip from the garage cleaning.

"Hey, you made it!" he exclaims cheerfully when he sees us.

"Yeah, I came to get my car," I say.

"Tristan thought it smelled like dog," Erik giggles. "But I thought it smelled like home."

"Geez, you're really struggling with the cleaning," Jenny says teasingly. "You're going to lose ten kilos if you keep this up."

"Ah, I don't want to lose weight. I need to gain a few pounds so that Ninni will fall in love with me," Erik says, laughing.

"But stop it now," I say, playfully punching him in the stomach.

A few days earlier, I had talked to Natalie on the phone and somehow managed to comment that Mitch was getting a little round in the body. When she pointed out that I was on speakerphone, I tried to compensate by saying that I love fat men, that I'd slept with several. My explanation didn't make him feel any less insulted, but my long-established social clumsiness became a topic of conversation that my friends—and apparently even superficial acquaintances—now entertain each other with.

It just clicks. Suddenly, Erik is looking at me like I'm some sort of desirable object, and I see him in a whole new light. I've always had trouble distinguishing between jokes and sincerity. When someone tells me something true, I have a hard time believing it; but I can easily read into things that aren't even remotely truthful. Even though I can rationally see that Erik is just being his usual attention-seeking self, in that moment, he becomes someone who could be attracted to me. It's happened before, many times. And it never goes anywhere. I want to be with Nathan, but after fourteen years together, I need occasional periods of validation from others. Now, I'm thinking that Erik could be one of those people. He's not that short, I think to myself. Above all, he's very funny. And intelligent. And obviously quite fond of me.

I share my thoughts with my best friends over our daily morning coffee chats: Natalie, Jenny, and Marisa. My relationship with them is what gets me through the day. Breakfast after dropping off the kids, lunch as a break, coffee before pickup, and an endless stream of conversations in between. We are a union of three different contexts. Jenny and I are neighbors who have slowly and carefully become friends. I've gone from seeing her as just kind and caring to one of the funniest and smartest people I know. She's instinctively maternal and incredibly protective of those close to her, mildly disdainful and critically dismissive of those she doesn't understand. She's either one or the other, and I'm glad to have her on my side. I wouldn't want her on the other side, because then she's quite merciless.

Natalie is originally from Gothenburg, a friend of Nathan's. When she and her husband moved to our street, we started hanging out pretty much immediately. I was instinctively hesitant, unattracted to Natalie's boundaryless nature and constant need for attention. But when we were alone, I saw that she was warm, caring, and undoubtedly one of the smartest people I've ever met. We bonded over our mutual interest in people and the world. Everyone always says that Natalie is one of the funniest people they know, but for me, she's primarily the wisest. She's the one whose advice I listen to the most. I trust that she knows me and always knows what's best for me, and I see her as my closest friend.

And then there's Marisa. At first, I called her a happy golden retriever because she's so uncritical of her surroundings. I thought her openness made her stupid, but now I know it makes her a better person. And she's definitely one of the funniest people I know. She may look like a blonde suburban mom on the surface, but she can deck anyone with her life stories. She's completely fearless and curious about everything and everyone. These three are my laughter, my every day, my relief, and my comfort. We are everything to each other that life and everyone else isn't. I couldn't survive without them, and they couldn't survive without me.

Our neighborhood is like a small village framed by the whitewashed, sugar cube-shaped homes and a row of pear trees. Here, everyone is moderately happy (it's still possible to make lighthearted jokes about our spouses' shortcomings), moderately environmentally conscious (of course, we should have an electric car, but not at the expense of the practicality of a seven-seater SUV, which is needed to drive the kids and their friends to activities, parties, outings, and sports days), moderately cosmetically enhanced (perhaps just a little something to deal with that migraine wrinkle on the forehead), and moderately athletic (enough to keep our bodies in shape, but not so much that we look worn out). In other words, it's a completely ordinary upper-middle-class utopia. Everyone thinks they're different, but really, we're all the same. Every morning after dropping off our kids at school and daycare, the stay-at-home moms gather to celebrate their children's and husbands' absence with coffee without pastries. So do we. Natalie, who just quit her job to become an entrepreneur, somewhat unclear about how, is in the middle of sharing a funny story about her husband. Jenny, who is also a freelancer but is currently on sick leave, nods her head and laughs at Natalie's relatable gripe. And then there's Marisa, who is on maternity leave with her newly started business, half-listening while she spoon-feeds carrot puree into little Turner's mouth. I sit down with an exhausted grunt, wondering how I'll manage to resist ordering a pastry with my coffee.

I give in and order a croissant with my coffee, ignoring Natalie's amused look when I bring the tray over. Natalie always thinks I eat too much, probably because I always feel like I'm eating too much. As I quickly devour my croissant, we move on to local gossip about people we know and those we know a little less. Erik comes up.

"He's actually funny," I say. "The kind of guy I could fall in love with."

Jenny looks at me in shock, and I think it's probably not the right time to tell her that I've already started walking the dog in the neighborhood around his house.

"Nah, he looks like a little gnome!" she exclaims, horrified.

But Natalie agrees with me. Erik is attractive. Smart and funny. Of course, Natalie thinks like I do. We like the same things.

The conversation continues. We discuss today's upcoming tasks, yesterday's anxieties, and tomorrow's possibilities, finish our coffee, and head home.

When I was twenty-two years old, I started working for a friend of my dad's. Michael was twenty-eight and ran the company with his girlfriend. He was extremely flirtatious. It affected me strongly. The attention. The jokes. The desire. After a long, gray, and depressive teenage period where I mostly waited for a life that never happened, Michael came along as if on cue. And the cynical, scared, and negative person that I was, and that I had nourished with my friends for so long, began to change. Due to a whole year of digestion issues, I lost my teenage weight. I dyed my hair blonde and started wearing tight clothes. At work, everyone talked about sex. And about how gorgeous I was. I became happy, outgoing, and, according to my old friends, changed my personality and became very superficial. I wasn't superficial—I was manic. I was obsessed with Michael and the feelings he gave me. In the shadow of that, nothing else mattered. That he was my dad's friend. That I worked side by side with his girlfriend every day. That I could see the dysfunctional reflection of myself in my friends' eyes but couldn't grasp what it meant. I lost them then. My two best friends since middle school, Lindsay and Gretchen, disappeared. Lindsay just slowly drifted away. She didn't understand me anymore. She didn't understand Michael or who I was for loving him. Gretchen was more direct. She invited me out to dinner and talked and talked about why she couldn't be my friend anymore until I cried all over my dessert and begged to go home.

Michael and I had sex for the first time when I was twenty-three. It was a morning on the floor of his girlfriend's office. She worked at their store in town at that time where she regularly cheated with other men over the internet. I knew that, but Michael didn't. This was my first time. First intercourse, first oral sex, the second person I had kissed since I was fourteen. I remember it being good. That whole period is very characterized by sexual drive, and I thought I was very much in love with Michael.

After it was over, I truly thought I was going to fall apart. I got a high fever. Lost 10 kg. And as it always is, a weekend, about three months later, I visited friends in London, was courted by a guy, and got over Michael at the same moment. Some years later, we started talking again and possibly saw each other a bit. I don't actually remember. But he had lost his significance. After I got over him, I was never afraid of being hurt in the same way. Because I knew it would pass. But the important lesson in the story passed me by unnoticed. If you don't learn the first time or the second time, life will give you the same lesson over and over again until you learn.

A few days later, we're invited to our neighbor Susan's fortieth birthday party, which is surprising because Nathan and I have never socialized with her or her unsympathetic husband. Hazel and Erik, as well as Natalie and Mitch, are also invited. We have dinner at our house first, and I grill a big piece of salmon, even though Nathan hates it, because it's easy to make for a lot of people. It's a lovely and warm summer evening in early June, and Erik and I end up sitting next to each other. He has something I need. I want his attention so I can feel calm, feel confident. I want him to see me, laugh with me, and seek me out. Right now, when he's doing just that, I feel rewarded and a little hyper at the same time.

Susan's party is in her garden, with lots of people who all seem older than us, but probably are around my age. There are old men and women dancing to rock music and drinking fruity drinks with lots of ice. Susan has hired a tattoo artist who works from a small house in their garden, and the line outside is filled with middle-aged men and women who want to get a pattern, number, or symbol tattooed on their body. I keep Hazel company in line, because she has always wanted a tattoo, which is surprising. Hazel is not even close to middle-aged, but maybe a little bit crisis prone. We ran into each other with our dogs down by the meadow the other day, and she talked about how she and Erik are struggling. He works too much, and she's starting to lose hope. "He would never leave me, I know that" she said. "But I'm not as sure about myself. But then, who would I even meet?"

Now she's standing next to me in line, ready to finally decorate her thin wrist with a strand of stars. "My mom will kill me," she says, and I understand why. Hazel is not the type to get a tattoo. She's the type of person who always looks impeccable, wearing layers of clothes that cost as much as my last sofa. She's incredibly beautiful, and I always feel too tall and too clumsy next to her. But the line never ends, and eventually we give up on the tattoo. I wonder where Erik is. I haven't seen him, Natalie, or Mitch in at least an hour now. When we find them on the lawn, we all stand in a circle with our arms around each other's shoulders.

"Can't we leave?" I say. "I just want to be with you guys."

"Yeah!" Hazel yells. "Let's go to our place and have an after-party."

I, who hate after-parties and always prefer to go to bed, now want nothing more than to go to their place and continue the party. But Nathan feels he must go home and relieve the babysitter, so only Hazel, Erik, Mitch, Natalie, and I go. Nathan got an electric bike for his fortieth birthday, which looks like a moped and is called Rawbike, and Erik takes Hazel home on it. Natalie, Mitch, and I walk. Fortunately, their kids are asleep by the time we get there, and we sit on the terrace facing the garden. Mitch puts on some music, and I dance happily by myself, barefoot on the soft wooden floor. I know I can't dance, but I rarely care. I move to what I perceive as the rhythm and don't think too much about what others see. However, Erik, who sits on the steps rolling a joint, looks at me appreciatively. Maybe he thinks I look funny. Maybe he thinks it's great that I'm having fun. At that moment, it doesn't matter because I feel good. I sit down next to Erik and Hazel, and we share the joint in silence. Mitch doesn't dare to smoke because he's afraid it might have a bad effect with his antidepressant medication. The fact that Erik, Hazel, and I have all been taking the same substance for years doesn't calm him. Hazel disappears, saying she needs to check on the kids, Natalie and Mitch stand a little further away dancing, and Erik and I are left alone on the steps. Now it doesn't feel okay anymore. It doesn't feel funny or harmless, but rather genuinely reckless. I feel an energy between us that I haven't felt with anyone other than Nathan in years. I shouldn't be here. And Nathan is at home with our children. Nathan, who never wants the party to end, is the one who went home, and here I am, smoking weed with someone who I suddenly realize could cross the line. When Erik goes to check on Hazel, I feel relieved and disappointed at the same time. But when he takes a while to come back, I tell Natalie and Mitch that we should go home because the people who live here have gone to bed. We get stuck at Nathan's Rawbike because the lock refuses to cooperate. We all try, but it won't budge. Probably more due to our state of mind than the lock. In the middle of our efforts, I see Erik standing on the steps laughing at us.

"I thought you fell asleep," I say.

"No, I just wanted to check on Hazel," he says. "How's it going for you guys?"

"This damn thing won't work," Mitch says.

"Maybe you should try turning the key," Erik suggests.

That did the trick, and soon we're all cycling home in a serpentine pattern over the entire road. I fall asleep with a bucket next to my bed, slightly panicked because I feel a little drunk.

When summer comes, I leave with some separation anxiety. It's been so much fun lately. New people, lots of parties, and an overall flirtatious atmosphere. Life at home feels alive and young. Nathan and I bought a summer house on Gotland, and now we're spending our first full summer here. We have visitors almost every day. It's lovely, but intense. And it leaves little room for our relationship—we're never alone with each other. Our big Rhodesian Ridgeback, Emma, is pseudo-pregnant after the longest heat ever, and I have to drag her along the gravelly paths in the blazing sun every day. It's a record-breaking hot summer, and Sweden is on fire. Literally. On my birthday, I get a notification that Erik has accepted my friend request on Facebook. It's been lying dormant for a while, and I instinctively and immediately respond:

"Finally! As a birthday present."

He responds with a joke that he timed it perfectly.

It should have ended there. But it didn't, and I respond. And he responds back. I know it was inappropriate. When he sends me the world's longest message with examples of events and people referencing the number forty-two, my age, and asking how often I get to experience the fruits of life. I know I need to stop. He's always walking a tightrope, it's just his personality and he's like that with everyone, but when he's with me and I'm doing the same thing, we become two kids playing with matches.

11

IN WITH THE NEW, OUT WITH THE OLD

The summer continues with friends, wine, and children in the pool. Natalie joins us for stretches with the kids while Mitch is busy traveling with work. She becomes an extra family member in our home. She was always a welcome, invited, and natural part of our family.

Together, we spend all holidays, weekends, and everything in between. We plan vacations around each other's schedules, and our kids are best friends. For a while, we lived on the same street, Natalie and Mitch's family in a small, terraced house, Jenny and Danny with their kids in a similar one, side by side with us. Susan and Robert in a third box, and Massimo and Stephanie in a house around the corner. The kids loved it—and so did we. The grill was always on, everyone's home was everyone's, and we ran between our houses to borrow milk or a bottle of wine, often staying for dinner. More people were called in or dropped by, and soon the house was bursting with sugar-stuffed children and wine-drunk adults. When Nathan and I sold our house to Ben and Sheila and moved a few blocks away, the intensity of our interactions was reduced for a while, but our presence in each other's lives is still constant. But with Erik's and Hazel's arrival, everything changes.

When autumn comes, Ben invites me and Nathan, but not Jenny and Natalie, to celebrate Sheila's birthday, which is the first hint of a rift between us. They were invited last year. And not us. What does this mean? Why is Ben grooming us, the other wonder. But Nathan and I are happy to be included, and we, along with two other couples, go out to celebrate Sheila with dinner and a music festival. One of the other couples is Hazel and Erik. I hate all types of concerts but am not entirely surprised to find myself thrilled at the idea of being close to Erik. He, Ben, and I get separated from the others during the performance. Hand in hand, we push through the crowd, hoping to find them. I don't want to. I hope I get to hold Erik's hand instead of Ben's.

"Should we ditch this and go to a bar instead?" Ben asks.

The three of us pile into the back of a taxi, me in the middle. My knee is close to Erik's, but he doesn't seem to notice.

Two weeks later, the same group goes to the coast to fish for lobster. Erik, Hazel, Nathan, and I share a car down, and Hazel has to sit in the front because she gets carsick. In the backseat, during a total of twelve hours of driving, I fall in love with Erik. But I'm not worried. I've fallen in love before during my marriage to Nathan and nothing ever happens. A little extra attention, the swelling pride of feeling seen, funny, beautiful, and alive is nice for a while, then it passes, and Nathan and I continue our life together. But in the front seat, Nathan and Hazel are also falling in love. And I don't notice anything at all.

The weekend away is a success. We stay at a beautiful hotel, and Hazel and I are up first every morning and have breakfast because we're early birds, unlike the others. Then we walk around the island, and when Erik is not holding Hazel's hand, he follows me, teasing me for various weaknesses. I giggle with delight, flattered by his devoted attention. We stop at the cliffs, the wind is cold, but the sun is shining, and Erik swims in the sea, even though it's October. So typical of Erik, says Hazel. When we go out to catch lobster, we all have to put on blue, oversized fishing suits that make us look like Stockholmers on a luxury tour. Hazel has to take photos for her blog, and Erik and Nathan take turns taking pictures of her with a lobster in her hand. Saltwater blows in my face, the boat rocks, and on the way back, we all lie in the bow and look at the sky. In the evening, we enjoy our self-caught lobsters, which are probably lobsters that someone else caught. And then we drink wine. A lot of wine. I sit next to Erik, who curiously rummages through my bag. He fishes out my ADHD medication that I have with me, even though I don't take it because I don't believe I have ADHD.

"What does this do?" Erik asks, holding up a tablet between his thumb and forefinger.

"It's a central stimulant that should have a calming effect on those whose brains spin too fast, I guess," I reply.

Erik quickly swallows the tablet with a glass of wine, and we all hold our breath, but it doesn't matter because no one notices any difference in Erik afterward anyway.

After dinner, we head down to the basement and drink more wine, dancing to Hazel's favorite songs played by Erik. We move on to a nearby bar, where we meet some friends from Gothenburg and Erik strikes up a conversation with the elderly locals on the patio. The rest of us head back, but Hazel can't get into their room because Erik has the keys. I offer to go get them. I don't know why I'm the one who has to do it, but I do it anyway. When I return to the patio, Erik is still there, deeply engrossed in intense conversations with the older couple.

"I think your wife and my husband want to sleep with each other," I say, and the old lady bursts out laughing.

"Great," Erik says with a grin, "then you and I have to have sex too."

I don't know what it is between us. But it's something. Maybe Erik just goes on autopilot with everything he says, but I take it seriously. Everything is said in jest, but it feels real. And I'm falling more and more in love. On the way back, Hazel sits up front next to Nathan who's driving, and Erik and I sit in the back. When we finally pull up to their house, Erik looks at me and says he could have stayed in the car forever. Probably because he's tired and hungover and it's nice to ride in a car, but I think he means he wants to sit in the backseat next to me.

Life happens quickly sometimes. The years after Nathan and my crisis felt slow and long, and I had started to long for some kind of chaos again, to feel something for real. The strongest feeling is when life takes on a life of its own and I lose control. When everything becomes chaos. And that's probably what I've been longing for when Erik and Hazel entered our lives. For three months, Nathan and I almost completely swap out all our friends for Hazel and Erik, sometimes Ben and Sheila. Jenny, Danny, Natalie, and Mitch withdraw more and more. We don't care because we're so completely preoccupied with falling in love with each other. Dinner at Erik and Hazel's, dinner at ours, wine lunches, Sunday walks with the dogs, planning for fall break, Easter break, and summer break, and a constantly flowing text thread between the four of us. Elise becomes best friends with Hazel and Erik's oldest daughter, and they take turns sleeping over at each other's houses. Life is boundless, intoxicating, and hopelessly enchanting.

But people are talking about Nathan and Hazel. That they might be in love. Erik sees it, too, and he's jealous and suspicious, but I dismiss it because I can't see any possibility of Nathan falling for Hazel. The one Nathan would leave me for is a lawyer, combative with classic style and a pearl necklace. Not young Instagram influencer with a children's clothing store. No chance. I don't see that when Erik and I sit and bicker in our corner, Hazel and Nathan are planning a new future in theirs. But one evening, when Hazel comes to our house to pick up a jacket her daughter forgot, I see it. Hazel and I are standing in the hall talking, and after a while, Nathan comes. When he turns his back to get the jacket, I see Hazel's gaze follow him. It's soft. And a little hungry. She's in love with Nathan. I almost giggle, and after dinner, I bring it up to him.

"I think Hazel might have a bit of a crush on you," I say, smiling at Nathan knowingly.

Nathan takes a sip of wine, tilts his head, and smiles back. "Well, of course, I am pretty fantastic. Are you worried?"

"No, not really," I say honestly. "We're in a good place right now."

Are we really in a good place, though? We're living our lives through other people while we renovate our summer house. We're running forward and backward at the same time. But am I worried? No, not about Nathan and Hazel. Not about me and Erik. Not about me and Nathan.

One night it happens, though. By accident. An accident that many of us, myself included, saw coming for a long time. But Erik is completely shocked by what he's capable of when we're both too drunk. The aftermath, at least for Erik, is monumental.

"I know you might not believe this, but I've never done anything like this before," he says. "I never thought I could be unfaithful to Hazel."

He disappears for a week. I don't hear from him. But when he's on a business trip in Norway, he sends a picture of himself in new sunglasses to our group chat. I call him.

"I just want to say that if you tell Hazel, she'll tell Nathan, and nothing good will come out of it."

"I have no plans to tell Hazel" he replies. His voice is metallic. "She and I have our own problems now, but they have nothing to do with what happened between you and me. I don't attach any emotional value to what happened between us," he concludes.

I'm not sure if I attach any emotional value to what happened either, but I know it never would have happened if I didn't have feelings for him. His words feel like small, sharp drills in my chest. And when we hang up, I cry violently.

But the next time we see each other, something seems to have clicked inside him. We're at dinner at Erik and Hazel's. Everyone is singing, drinking, smoking, and playing guitar. The kids must be somewhere, but I don't know where. Erik is too much. Too obvious. He puts his feet on my lap as if he and I were together, and I feel uncomfortable. I think Hazel sees it. I step out with her for a smoke.

She takes a deep breath. Several times, she's about to say something, but when I ask what, she says, "It's nothing."

Erik comes out, and Hazel goes in. Hazel always leaves us alone. He stands one step below me, so he's even shorter than usual. Erik looks at me and squints.

"Are we okay?" he wonders.

I say hesitantly, "Yeah, why wouldn't we be?"

He grins broadly. "I thought what happened between us was fun," he says.

I don't understand what he means and go back inside with the others. But Erik follows me everywhere, saying that there's nothing to worry about, that we're just in love. It's nothing strange. He's very drunk.

When I go home, he texts me. He's intense, saying that I seduced him and that I'm continuing to flirt with him by touching my neck so gently when I talk to him. Then he tells me to come over.

I don't respond, but he continues to text me that I'm teasing him, that I manipulated him, and that I need to come over. I turn off my phone and fall asleep, but when I wake up, he has called me three times. I'm angry and terrified.

I send him a message: "You can't call me. What if Nathan had seen? You must stop this. This is not a new deal."

But that's exactly what it is, and day by day, it only gets worse. I never think that I'm going to leave Nathan for Erik. I think it's something that will pass. But it doesn't pass, it gets worse. And the last time we have sex, something shifts inside. It's different. Erik says it was like we were making love, and maybe we were. I don't know, but I know that I now have a hard time looking Nathan and Hazel in the eye. It's starting to feel unbearable. So, we decide to stop talking. But two days later, it's New Year's Eve, and we're all going to celebrate together.

Hazel and I have planned everything. We and way too many others have rented out a small hotel by the sea for a private celebration. It's primarily used as a conference hotel and comes complete with a spa and sauna. The kids are ecstatic and run around like little excited puppies, exploring every corner of the hotel. The decor is dark with moss-green walls, wooden details, and pine tables and chairs. Some of us adults gather in the sauna. Nathan isn't there, but Erik and Hazel are. Hazel's face is covered in a green cream that dries to a face mask.

"It's supposed to refresh my skin," she explains.

"Yes, you look very refreshing," Erik says enthusiastically and looks playfully at her, but Hazel looks away.

Some people leave the sauna to cool off in the sea just outside the door, and Erik asks Hazel if she wants to join, but she doesn't. I sit quietly and don't enjoy the heat. I don't really like saunas. Hazel and Erik's son Cole comes in and asks if anyone wants to swim with him, and Hazel offers to go with him.

"But you didn't want to swim before," Erik says.

"I didn't before, but I do now," Hazel replies.

I observe their conversation and Erik's familiar futile pursuit of Hazel's love and approval with a slight feeling of anxiety in my stomach. I recognize this dance so well. Nathan and I danced around each other like this for years, always with him just out of reach from my attempts to get closer. But I can't feel sorry for Erik because in his attempts to get closer to Hazel, he's also moving further away from me.

The sauna empties out, and eventually, it's just Erik and me left. Erik and I don't talk to each other. I don't know how to be normal with him now that we're not supposed to have any contact. Now that we're supposed to pretend that nothing happened, and I sit beside him, watching him struggle to make his wife love him. So, I leave, and Erik is left alone in the sauna.

I'm not doing well. I'm hiding in my hotel room and wishing I were somewhere else. I've bought an overly expensive dress, which I put on over my now too-thin body. Then I go up to join the others for dinner. Hazel has arranged the seating and I sit between Erik and Ben on one side of the table, while Nathan and Hazel sit together on the other. Earlier, when Erik and I talked, we joked about him touching me under the table. That we'll have sex in one of the hotel rooms. Because we can't stay away from each other. But now we can't even talk. I'm silent, and Erik talks with a loud metallic voice, not even looking at me. It's a relief when dinner is over and I can join others. I mostly hang out with Ben, clinging to him like a security blanket.

Erik is off in a room with Sheila, crying over Hazel. I'm everywhere and nowhere. I want to be everywhere except here. At home, my real friends are celebrating the new year at Marisa's place. They have warmth, thoughtfulness, and love. I'm wearing an expensive dress and have nowhere to go. I want to be where Erik is. But he's always somewhere else.

Ben and I find him and Sheila in a room with glass walls. I press my face against the glass to get a reaction. Sheila shakes her hands and says, "No, this is not the time."

Erik looks at me with disgust and quickly looks away. I go in and sit on a chair. I hear Sheila talking to a sad Erik about his marriage. I leave and return to the party with the others. I dance with Hazel until Sheila comes up looking grim and takes her hastily down the spiral staircase. Her long silk dress flows behind her like a cloak.

I wake up early the next morning and go down to the kitchen. Only a few are awake, and Erik is making scrambled eggs. Cole is climbing on the tables, and Hazel is sitting with a tight-lipped face at a table, trying not to look at him, but eventually losing it and screaming at him to get down. I wonder why Hazel is so angry. Something must have happened the night before. I wonder what Erik has said. Sleepy and hungover people fill the room, and Erik whistles loudly in the kitchen. He serves us all scrambled eggs, which he doesn't eat. Instead, he goes up to his room, still whistling.

I'm heading home as fast as I can. Nathan and I went there in two cars, so I take one and he and the kids can come after. He thinks I'm abandoning them, but I need to get out of there. Now. I stop by a lake, kneel next to the car, smoke, and cry all the tears I couldn't cry yesterday.

12

THE SWITCH

Total silence from everyone. Nobody knows anything. Nobody says anything. I take Emma for a walk and run into Hazel with her dogs.

"Well, hello," I say, slightly surprised.

"Hi," Hazel says in a low voice.

"How's it going?" I wonder, eager to know what's going on between her and Erik.

"Oh, it's chaos. I've moved out, I'm staying with my mom and dad." Hazel looks both sad and relieved at the same time.

"But what . . . what happened? Was it the argument on New Year's Eve?"

I haven't talked to Erik, so I don't know what happened. Except that he served everyone a perfect scrambled egg breakfast on New Year's Day morning, in a great mood, while Hazel was super upset.

"No, but maybe divorce, I don't know," she says, suddenly looking very sad.

I get anxious. None of this was supposed to be real. Nothing was supposed to have consequences. Now everything has consequences.

Erik is completely devastated. He says we can't talk anymore because I draw attention away from his relationship with Hazel. I say I don't know what's happening, but I want to treat my and Nathan's relationship with respect and give us the time we need to get through this. So Erik and I decide, maybe for the seventh time, that we won't talk anymore. It doesn't last very long. Erik texts me from London where he's lying in bed crying and listening to "Delirious" by Susanne Sundfør. My power song, which he now makes his own. He says Hazel is harsh and cold and that she's crushing him. He crushes me when he says that. He says I give him strength and energy. Then I feel like a light bulb.

I text Erik and say we have to stop talking. That he has to figure out his own stuff. I have enough problems on my plate. That he needs to sort out his issues with Hazel and himself and stop using me as a sounding board and comfort blanket.

He gets angry and replies that I need to stop acting like a victim and realize that we're in this together. That he doesn't want to discuss Hazel with me—he wants to be with me. And not as a security blanket.

Confirmation and hesitation, like a hug with a punch in the gut. Because I can't think that it's not real. I can't feel and have distance to what I feel at the same time. So, when the words sink in, all I feel is the hug and the strokes along my back. I don't see any red flags or warning signs. I, who broke up with my first boyfriend for self-preservation, suddenly have no boundaries. Only Erik's words exist.

But we decide not to talk anymore. I go to Gothenburg because I can't take it anymore. I can't handle my friends who are worried about my mental state. I can't handle Erik who wants to talk about his relationship, whether it's there or not, with me. And the decision he says he has to make. I, who have already made my decision with or without a future with Erik, can't be a sounding board. Or a victim. So I go back home and wake up in my mom's guest room to a text from Erik. He tells me that Hazel admitted that she has feelings for Nathan and she thinks they're mutual.

I still doubt that they're mutual. But I understand that Erik must be in shock. Especially when he tells me that he dragged Hazel out and threw her out on the stairs. He refused to let her in, and in the end, their daughter had to open the door. Shock reaction, he explains. I don't react much to his reaction. I'm too focused on what it means for his feelings for me to think about what it says about his feelings for Hazel.

When I come home, there's a wall between Nathan and me. That old wall. Nathan goes up to put the kids to bed, and when he comes down, he sits across from me on the couch and says we need to talk.

"About what?"

"About you and Erik and me and Hazel," he replies, looking at me with an unwavering gaze.

So, we talk. We don't talk much about what happened, but more about how we feel. And we quickly decide to visit our old family therapist again. The one who always put us on separate bridges so the other could speak uninterrupted. When we're there, I tell it like it is, that I'm madly in love with Erik. And Nathan admits that he's in love with Hazel. As we sit in the car on the way home, there's a soft, silent understanding between us. I break the silence.

"What just happened?"

"I think we just decided to separate," Nathan says. "But whatever happens, we will treat each other with respect. You will always be a part of me, and you are my best friend."

I agree. Nathan isn't going anywhere. He's just moving aside a bit. We'll continue together, just on different paths. I tell myself that I'm not getting divorced to be with Erik, but it's the feelings I have for him that give me the strength to leave. It's what makes it okay to be left. I feel too strongly about Erik to feel anything else. I'm not being cheated on, lied to, or deceived. We're even. And that means we can leave each other as friends.

Erik and I meet in the parking lot of Plantagen. He bought a chandelier tree, with crystal flowers swaying heavily in Erik's hand.

"Well, I had to buy something since I said I was going to Plantagen." Erik laughs because he didn't tell Hazel that we're meeting.

They still live together, just like Nathan and me. I sit next to Erik in their car, and "Don't You (Forget About Me)" plays on the radio, while Erik asks me where we should go on vacation.

"I don't know where we'd go, we have completely different interests," I say. "I hate skiing."

"Well, I'll get you over that." Erik smiles.

I, who promised myself I'd never stand on a ski slope again, think that with Erik, it might be possible. I long to discover the world together with him. It feels like anything is possible.

"Everything feels both terrible and fantastic at the same time," Erik says.

I, who haven't been cheated on or left, just think it feels fantastic.

We go to a café and drink tea in big mugs and giggle over our shared secret. Everything feels magical. Erik's usually chubby body is now very slim. We don't talk about Hazel and Nathan. Not yet. We're interesting enough to each other to be able to meet without thinking about anything else.

There are few things that can compare to diving deep into another person with all that you are. Letting yourself be consumed, overwhelmed, and swallowed whole so that the world becomes hazy and the only thing that's sharp is him. Our longest phone call lasts for six hours. We mute the phone when we pee. We each make dinner and drink too much wine from our respective empty divorce homes. We send each other photos of ourselves as children and as teenagers. We talk about first love, big love, the love that never was, our parents, our siblings, our children, our innermost thoughts. And I fall in love with Erik for real. Because he's not at all shallow and cold, but deep, passionate, with swirling thoughts and emotions that flow over and into me between our phone calls.

"You and I have both married each other's opposites," he says. "But that doesn't necessarily have to be a bad thing. The likelihood of it working out between you and me—with a clean switch—is incredibly small."

My heart sinks. He's everything I want. After spending years trying to guess what Nathan feels and thinks, Erik is an open book. I think it means that he is an empathetic and emotional man. One who can make me happy.

"But—" he says, making a small opening between his thumb and index finger. And I can breathe again.

It could work, I think. It could be good. A life that is real, with real emotions, ups and downs can be mine. I have it right in front of me.

I'm out walking in the woods with Emma when we first approach the subject of what we actually are. Because we're not together. We're not even divorced yet.

"But can we sleep with others?" I ask, who would never want to sleep with anyone else.

Erik hesitates. I can't breathe.

"No, I don't think so," he says, and I can breathe.

I'm generally bad at sleeping with multiple people at the same time. I have a hard time separating sex and love. I apologize for it with my late sexual debut. And my few serious relationships. Nathan is the only serious relationship I've had. And the question is how serious it is when you can't say that you love each other and, moreover, later find out that one partner was never in love with you. Erik tells that me over lunch. We sit around the kitchen table with a plate of untouched pasta in front of us when he shares the knowledge that Nathan said he was never really in love with me. I start to cry. He says he told me because he cares about me. He says that if he were me, he would want to know. He is remorseful and asks for forgiveness, but it hurts just the same.

I ask Nathan as soon as I get a chance. We're swapping houses and children and Nathan is standing at the sink rinsing off a plate when I say, "Erik says that Hazel has told him that you've told her that you were never in love with me. That they were at least in love, unlike us."

Nathan freezes, familiarly. He takes a new plate and rinses it carefully. "That's very difficult for me to imagine saying," he says.

I don't believe him, but I don't know why I need to know. Maybe we've never been in love. Maybe we never loved each other. Maybe we were just friends who started a family together. Right now, I think it might be true. Because I've forgotten what it felt like those first few years when I was super in love with him. Right now, all I can think about is how in love I am with Erik. Who says he's a little in love with me.

During the winter break, Jenny, Danny, Natalie, Mitch, Nathan, and I, and all our children are going on vacation to Sri Lanka. Nathan and I think we can travel together with the children, despite being separated. We're friends. No one is angry at the other. Struck by a sudden fearlessness for things I've always wanted to do but never dared, I decide to get my diving certification before we leave. Mitch and a third guy, Mateo, who is also going on the trip, are taking it with me. The final dive will be in Sri Lanka. It's an intensive course with exams and diving over three days. The dive exam is done in a large indoor pool, outside of the city, and it goes well. There are a lot of instructions, and I'm really bad at listening and doing as they say. Especially scary is when you have to take off your mask under the water and then put it back on. I get a mouthful of water every single time. But I managed it. With wet hair and a partial diving certificate, I leave the building to reach my car, parked a bit away. It had snowed a lot while we were inside the swimming hall, and I can't find my car. They all look the same, buried in a foot of snow. I walk around the parking lot once, then again. On the fifth lap, I start to cry. I call Nathan, but he shows no sympathy and finds it highly unlikely that the car is actually gone.

"Take a taxi home," he says.

I get furious and hang up. I call Erik, who's at a restaurant with his friend Lars, drinking wine and can't possibly come and get me. He's surprised and amused that I lost my car. "Take a taxi home," he advises.

I hang up and cry uncontrollably. The snow is so deep, and I'm carrying my diving equipment and that of others, for some reason that I've taken responsibility for. I feel like I'm the loneliest and most lost person in the world. After walking around the parking lot for an hour and a half, I call Natalie. She's so calm on the phone. She's the only one who understands me, I think.

"Take a taxi here right away," she advises. I do it. The next day, when Erik reluctantly drives me to look for the car, we find it right away.

A week before the trip, Natalie comes over to my house for dinner while Nathan stays at Hazel's place. Erik calls and wants to come by to pick up his daughter who is playing with Elise at our place. I say okay. Nathan has been very clear on one point, which is that he doesn't want Erik and me to meet in the house. It's Nathan's house, after all, and he's the one who will continue to live here even though I still reside here. He doesn't want it tainted by me and Erik together. But he can stand in the hallway, I think. When Erik arrives, he wonders if he can come in for a glass of wine while waiting for his daughter to want to come home. "Surely that's okay," I think.

Natalie becomes very uncomfortable. She knows I promised Nathan that Erik wouldn't be in the house, and she doesn't understand how I could do the opposite. After a while, Natalie goes home, and Erik and I have sex in the garden, on the cold stone steps up to the front door. Not in the house, in other words. *Surely, that's okay?*

But of course, it's not.

Natalie tells Nathan about my misstep pretty soon, and at Jenny's place, he, Natalie, and Jenny discuss the trip to Sri Lanka and what Nathan should do. He is terribly angry with me. Natalie and Jenny advise him to tell me that I shouldn't come along since the two of us will risk ruining everyone's vacation together under the same roof now that Nathan is so furious with me. It's not good for the children either. And I probably just want to be with Erik anyway, they reason. So, I have to stay home.

It was my suggestion, after all. That I should be the one to stay home and Nathan should go, considering that he's the one who can afford it, not me. He agrees, and with my best friends, he goes on vacation with the children. Once there, he seems to feel guilty and bombards me with pictures of them all in the surf until I ask him to stop.

Nathan and I have rented a time-share in the area. Erik also stays there when he's not traveling, and Nathan never stays there since he and Hazel live in her parents' apartment when I'm at the house with the kids. Erik and I have dinners together, never breakfast because Erik is sleeping, and he doesn't eat breakfast anyway. Sometimes he does it just for company. Mostly we drink wine and talk and talk and talk. I want to know everything about him. He wants to know everything about me. We sit at the narrow table opposite each other but on the same side, always on the same side, with our feet in each other's laps or around each other's joints. Erik, who has just returned from a work trip to Paris, suddenly says that, of course, we can sleep with others.

"But you're the one who said we shouldn't do that," I protest, secretly panicked.

"I find it hard to believe I ever said that," he says with the voice he has when he forgets that he's lying. The way people talk without breathing. "We're not together. We're undefined."

Are we in love? I don't know because I'm afraid to talk. But Erik is in crisis, and I'm waiting.

For years, I have longed for an emotional, vulnerable, and transparent person, and now I am inundated with confessions about Erik's limited feelings for me, Erik's bitterness over Hazel's betrayal, and Erik's moralizing about her and Nathan's behavior, which I argue with Nathan about in the hopes that they will stop so that Erik will stop crashing every time it happens. I am a security blanket that asserts my integrity with hollow arguments about how it's the feeling that matters and not the words. It's the actions and all the times when Erik, during our hours-long, wine-filled conversations, shows me how important I am to him that matter, not that he says he feels disconnected the next day. So we create a pretend home in my exchange home. It's not renovated, but is an incredibly cozy house. When Erik isn't staying with his kids in his and Hazel's house or traveling, he stays with me. When he travels, we talk in the morning, at lunch, in the evening, and text in between. It's completely hypnotizing. But Erik isn't in love with me. He's disconnected, he says. Dead inside. I call Nathan and ask if he and Hazel say they are in love with each other.

"Yes, but aren't you in love too?"

"Erik says he can't say he's in love," I complain.

"No, but I think one should be able to say that now," says Nathan, who is just as clear as I am.

Nathan, Hazel, and I are all done with processed and completed marriages, but Erik hasn't caught up, he says. "I just need a little time to catch up," he says. And he feels so in love. The energy between us is intense and overwhelming. I feel seen and validated. And understood. Unlike Nathan, who has always said that life with me is a roller coaster of intense emotional outbursts and crises, Erik thinks I'm easy. And as long as you keep the same pace as the roller coaster, there are no problems.

"Ugh, it's so difficult," I say. "It's so damn complicated to try to find each other in this mess of everything that has happened. Haven't you had a hard time, you and Hazel?"

Nathan is quiet and thinking. "No," he admits. "For us, it's actually been very easy all the way. It's so easy with Hazel. And it feels so natural."

Shallow assholes, I bitterly think. They have no feelings to take into account. They just roll on with their couple dinners and group drinks as if nothing has happened. Out with Ninni and Erik, in with Nathan and Hazel. They don't have what Erik and I have. We are complicated people with lots of layers of feelings and experiences to consider. We will have it so good when we get through all of this. We will have it so much better than them. We are real people who will meet in a genuine relationship where both are completely honest and constantly in touch with their feelings.

One Saturday after Erik had been to the pool with his children, he texts me and tells me about a funny incident that has happened. He had run into an acquaintance, a girl who one of his friends has tried to set him up with. He said it was so fun and lovely, and that he had been flirting with her. I ask him what he meant that he had flirted with her. I say I don't want to hear anymore. He asks if I'm jealous, and I say yes.

He goes silent and doesn't contact me until the next day, with a text saying hi.

"Do you want to hang out?" I try to sound casual, but I know something is up.

He says that he doesn't know if we should because of my reaction yesterday.

"Because I didn't want to small talk about you flirting with some girl at the pool?"

He says he didn't like that I said I was jealous, so I agree that we shouldn't meet.

I hesitate and then text him again. Just to make sure he truly is the asshole I think he is. "Just so I don't misunderstand here: you don't think we should meet because I got jealous = emotionally involved?"

"Yes."

"Okay, over and out."

I put the phone down trembling, sink to the floor, and start to cry. How did we end up here now? What could I have done differently? When was it decided that we couldn't be emotionally involved? Erik makes up his own rules for our relationship (which is a non-relationship if he gets to decide) as we go along. And I just go along with it. After a while, he calls and asks if he can still come over. He takes two steps into the hallway and hugs me. I cry.

"Little you, so wobbly," he says, stroking my hair. "What should we do with you?"

One Saturday in March, Marisa invites us to celebrate her birthday. Erik, Nathan, Hazel, and I are all invited. It's my and Erik's week with the kids, but I quickly switch days with Nathan so that I can go. And I urge Erik to do the same. I dream of us being able to go to a party together. I want everyone to see how fantastic he is. I want him to see how fantastic my friends are. I want him, instead of feeling like the loneliest person in the world, to feel surrounded by people who like him. That he has a context, despite his old context now being inhabited by Nathan. But Erik doesn't want to go. He has no babysitter, he says. I suggest several solutions, but he is indecisive. When there are only a few days left, he says that he has a babysitter. That his friend Daniel's girlfriend is going to look after his children so that he and Daniel can go out. I become so unsure that I don't even dare to ask why he doesn't want to go to the party. So we dance around what he and Daniel are going to do for a while until he finally says it was just a joke.

So, I go to the party alone. Just me with Natalie, Mitch, Jenny, and Danny. There are lots of people and strong drinks at Marisa and Adam's place. I get super drunk. I film myself in the bathroom when I bump into the mirror and send it to Erik.

"Come here instead," he says, and I go to his place.

The kids are sleeping, and we sit on the kitchen floor and talk. I'm drunk, and he's sober. I'm in love, and he's shut down. We have sex against the kitchen counter, and afterward, we sit on the floor, with my back against his chest, his arms around me. It should feel safe and warm and natural, but everything just feels even more wrong. And I start crying. Pretty hysterically. The crying is accompanied by hyperventilation, and suddenly, I'm in the middle of a panic attack. Erik just sits there quietly, holding me. Calm. Fearless. Safe. Then we fall asleep spooning on the couch. Erik sets the alarm so that we'll wake up before the kids, and he texts Jenny. She just spilled frozen blueberries all over Marisa's kitchen floor, thinking they were peas. She's anxious. But she also wonders if I'm okay. He's going to take care of me, he promises Jenny. I don't sleep through the night but wake up after an hour and go home. I'm calm, knowing that with Erik, I can be whoever I want. He's not afraid of my emotional loops. I'm safe with him, and he's going to take care of me, he says.

Ben and Sheila are having dinner on Friday, and I'm invited, but Erik won't let me go. He wants to make a point of not doing the same thing as Nathan and Hazel, who hurt him terribly by quickly socializing as a couple in social contexts. Erik thinks it's wrong and that it sends the wrong signals if he were to do the same thing.

"You and Sheila can, of course, invite whoever you want," he tells Ben. "But it's up to me to decide what I want, and it's not something you should worry about or think about. I don't think it's respectful to my and Hazel's historical relationship if Ninni and I go to dinner in a couple constellation," he finishes, not very pleased with his speech.

So Erik and I are not a couple, but we are also not allowed to go to the same dinner because then we would be seen as a couple. I understand Erik and go to dinner at Jenny and Danny's place instead. And when Erik is drunk, he texts me and asks if I can come over anyway. I gracefully decline, and he goes over to them instead. Danny is irritated.

"But you must understand that it's humiliating for Ninni that you forbid her from going to dinner," he says to Erik.

"I'm not forbidding her anything," Erik says with a blank face. "But then I can't go. I think it's unclean to socialize with my and Hazel's friends so close to our divorce."

"But Nathan and Hazel do it, don't they?" protests Jenny.

"Yes, exactly, and that's why I would never do the same thing."

As someone who is a little drunk, I don't feel like anything matters much anymore except for wanting to be where Erik is. So we leave Jenny and Danny and go over to Ben and Sheila's. I sit on the other side of the table and see how their friend talks long and eagerly with Erik. Afterward, he tells me that she had a friend she wanted to set him up with. I don't understand why he tells me this. And I don't understand why she thought Erik was available for a blind date. I don't understand why Erik didn't tell her, but I understand least of all why he tells me.

A couple of weeks later, Jenny, Natalie, and Marisa meet with me at my divorce apartment because they want to talk to me. We sit around the kitchen table. It feels like they have coordinated what to say.

"We're worried about you," Marisa says softly.

"It seems like your whole world is spinning super-fast. And why do you fight so much with Nathan all the time? He's really upset," Natalie says in a hard voice.

To me this sounds harsh. It's probably not meant to be, but Natalie is so clear and direct that I feel criticized. Natalie is one of Nathan's closest female friends and up until this period, my best friend. It's difficult. When everyone realized that Nathan and I were going to get divorced, Natalie said that I was her friend, first and foremost. Even though Nathan means a lot to her too. I understand that. I understand that it's difficult. But her words still hurt. And I always feel like she's taking his side, which in itself is so silly because my and Nathan's divorce barely has any sides. We both want to divorce. But somehow, it has become a competition in who does it more honorably. And honorable is not my strong suit. Nathan never acts on impulse. He is thoughtful, thorough, and conscientious. I have sex with my lover in the guest bathroom. I lose myself in fits of rage, martyrdom, and dissension. Nathan always wins. At least that's the truth I come up with as I sit and listen to my best friend explain how I'm doing. How I'm acting. And why it worries her. But I don't feel her worry. I only feel her criticism.

Natalie has explicitly taken a step away from me during this period. She has her own grief, her own relationships to figure out. And she's done. She doesn't have the energy to work. She doesn't have the energy to be a supportive friend. She doesn't have the energy for anything. I understand this. I don't know how many times I've told her that I do understand this. But it doesn't feel like I'm getting through. It feels like she always thinks I'm blaming her for her lack of presence in my life. And it's very possible that I am. I feel like an outsider. I don't understand why she has the energy to socialize with others, but not with me. I don't need her support, her advice, or her comfort. I just want someone to have dinner with. So I get angry.

"And poor, little Leo," Jenny says with blank eyes. "He's so worried about you. He has to take on so much, and he's so sensitive. It hurts me so much to see him try to protect you and take care of you. A child should not have to take on such responsibility."

No, certainly not. And I don't recognize myself in her description. I get angry and scream at all three of them. I say that it feels unsafe and not at all caring, and that I want them to leave. They go and I sit on the terrace and smoke. Again.

I call Erik and cry. He says that no one else but the two of us knows what is true between us and that I shouldn't listen to them. That Natalie is super-ego and Jenny is stupid and a bunch of other things that also makes me angry. Because they are my family. I can say they're stupid, but no one else can. I want Erik to like them because they're a part of me, and when he doesn't like them, it feels like he likes me even less.

My friends are probably right in everything they say. Everything is spinning so fast. A little chaos all the time. I lose cars, computers, car keys, but above all, I lose myself completely in the feeling of being with Erik. In the feelings of falling in lust and falling in love. Of being constantly desired, called, and close to someone who says he is shut down but doesn't act as such. He feels skinless, alive, and warm—just like me.

Nathan and I buy a townhouse for me and the children in what people call the "divorce row" because the houses there are some of the few in our expensive area that are economically accessible to us divorced people. I am moving in at the end of May and I am still staying in my shared accommodation when I'm at Jenny's celebrating her birthday. She is turning forty-five and we are all there, building champagne towers, eating cake, drinking cocktails, and I FaceTime with Erik. He is at Ben's summer place, playing tennis and getting high. He left yesterday. We saw each other the night before in the shared accommodation for the first time in a week because he had been on a business trip to Madrid. We talked unusually little during the trip, but when he comes home and we have sex on the hallway floor as soon as he comes in, I thought everything was still normal. After too much wine, Erik starts asking where we stand.

"What are we, really?" he wonders with a blurry gaze.

I hate this topic. Because I know I am in one place, and he is in another. So, I change the subject. The next day, he gets into the car to go to Ben's summer place. It is a warm spring day, and I am standing outside in a t-shirt with "Happy Endings" printed in capital letters all over my chest. Erik turns the car around and comes back for something he has forgotten. He says it was lucky because then he got to kiss me goodbye one more time. "So long, Happy Endings," he says, smiling warmly with a squint in his eyes and I feel like the happiest and most loved person in the world.

Now I am sitting in Jenny's garden FaceTiming with him and all of Ben's friends. They are not sober, and neither am I. Erik is giggly and loving on magic mushrooms, and I have a hard time hanging up. But Jenny is celebrating her birthday with all my best friends inside, so I hang up and go in. I take a picture of Natalie and me and send it to Erik. He takes a picture of himself in the woods and sends it back. As I'm on my way home, he calls again.

"But what are we, really?" he wonders once again.

"I don't know," I reply honestly and a little panicked. "I'm in the middle of a divorce and so are you. So, we're undefined, I guess."

"I can't see us as exclusive," he says suddenly.

"What do you mean?" I ask.

"Well, just so you don't think we're going to get married or anything," he says with a laugh.

I don't laugh. But I don't protest either. I continue talking to the image of Erik greedily devouring a large bucket of cold chicken while he continues to talk about all the things we are not.

The next morning, I wake up angry. I text him that I don't think his behavior was okay and that I do want us to be exclusive. He doesn't respond for several hours. Finally, I message him again and he replies with a long, cold message that stays with me for a long time.

He says that he really likes me and doesn't see me as just a casual fling, but he also feels a little lost and needs to take time to understand himself.

He says he doesn't want to hurt me, but he can't be exclusive if we're really undefined. He wants to keep his options open while he figures out what he really wants.

I reply that in that case we can't see each other anymore. And so, we stop seeing each other. Just like that. Again.

13

WELL, THIS WAS A REAL SHITSTORM

There is a big void after him. Or at least, I could be feeling it if I let myself feel. But instead I'm just chattering away to anyone who will listen. I'm lying on Jenny's couch, bawling my eyes out with exhausted Natalie next to me. I'm thinking it's all over. Jenny tells me she saw Erik, and apparently, he just needs some time. Ben tells her he's in love, but just hasn't figured it out yet. I'm thinking maybe everything will still be okay.

Nathan and I have sold all of our dreams of a generational summer home in Gotland. Jenny tags along with me to pack up everything the movers won't take. We rent a trailer and cram my dog Emma and ourselves into the car. Jenny does all the heavy lifting for three days while I smoke, cry, pack, and smoke some more. I can't eat. All I can do is cry, carry stuff, and smoke. When my past and future are packed away in the car, Jenny and I start driving back to catch the ferry. She turns to me with a smile.

"Now it's just you and me, and we're going to celebrate that this is over with a glass of wine," she says.

We find a restaurant near the port and sit outside with a glass of white wine each. I start feeling a bit hopeful, maybe it's just the wine, maybe it's Jenny being so nice, or maybe it's just knowing that it's all over: Nathan, Erik, life, etc. When it's time to go back to the ferry, Jenny heads to the bathroom. She's left a few sips of wine at the bottom of her glass, which I down greedily while she's gone. Then we get into the car and start the three-minute drive from the restaurant to the ferry terminal. I'm driving, and then the police pull us over for a sobriety check.

I pull up to them and blow into the breathalyzer. The police officer lifts his arm and yells to his colleague a few feet away.

"We have a match!"

And then everything happens really fast. The other police officer rushes up to my car, they tell me to get out, and they grab my arm as I try to reach in the back to get my license from my purse.

"Some people drink more alcohol to try and manipulate the test," one of the cops tells me.

And then I start bawling—not some quiet crying, but full-on ugly crying—while I dig out my license from my stuff. Emma's in the back, staring at me with her big, black, puppy dog eyes. The cops look mildly embarrassed.

"She's going through a divorce," Jenny hisses at them.

They nod sympathetically, but they still don't let go of my arm. I have to go to the police station. Jenny, who has about the same blood alcohol level as me—one glass of wine—takes the driver's seat, leaves the terminal with the car, trailer, and dog, and drives back to Stockholm on the ferry. And I follow the police officers to the station in town. They put me in the backseat, still crying. All my stuff is still in the car. I have my phone and my wallet, but no dignity. They let me make one call, and then they want my phone.

I call Nathan to tell him what happened. Poor Nathan. Trustworthy Nathan. He quickly gives me clear instructions: ask for a blood test, drink lots of water. A little while after we hang up, he texts me that he has booked a flight for me to go home a few hours later, and I feel a bit calmer, but I still can't stop crying.

The police station is a small stone house with natural-colored interior and small rooms, one for interrogating, one for changing and searching. A female police officer accompanies me into the latter to search me. My tears are a steady flow of now silent tears.

"Do you want a glass of water?" she asks, a little horrified by my pitiful state.

"No!" her colleagues from the adjoining room roar. "No water!"

Damn. No water. They know it can ruin any potential blood test.

I go with the two male officers into the interrogation room for my account of what happened. Where do I start? With Erik in November?

With Nathan at Christmas? Consumed by intense self-pity, I sob out the story of my divorce, my and Jenny's packing up the summer house, that one glass of wine I drank, and how terrible and incredibly sad it is that I ended up in this situation. Above all, how shameful it is. It's like all my actions in the past six months are summed up in this event. Our hour-long conversation is also accompanied by a drunken man in a neighboring cell who intermittently screams out his anguish. The officers shift uncomfortably after each scream and apologize if it's awkward. I've never felt sadder or more pathetic than at that moment in the police station. But the officers are so kind. One of them has just gone through his own divorce and says he understands. That it's terrible, but it will get better.

The meter has measured my breath alcohol content to a level of 0.1, which would correspond to 0.2 in the blood, if I were to take a blood test, which they recommend that I don't do and that I can't be bothered to do. I'm right on the edge, but still over, which means I get to keep my driver's license, but I'll have a record of drunk driving. The relief of keeping my license is minimal, and the shame of what's happening is overwhelming. When they're done, they drive me to the airport, and I finally get to go home. I call Nathan and he promises not to tell anyone what happened. "Stories like this have a way of spreading like wildfire," he says.

Back home in Stockholm, spring is in full bloom, and I have promised Elise and Carina, Erik's daughter, that we would go to Gröna Lund. Actually, it's Erik and I who promised them that, but now it's just me. We're going in the afternoon, and I go to a sushi restaurant for lunch first. When I sit on the outdoor terrace, Erik walks up the street, dressed entirely in black. He looks resigned when he sees me but asks if he can join me. I say yes, and that maybe it's good that we have an official conversation about how we ended things. He looks like he's been punched in the face. It's so strange that he always gets to be the victim. That he manages to combine shame with self-pity in one and the same look.

Afterward, I text him and ask if he wants to come with me, Elise, and Carina to Gröna Lund because I don't want to go alone and Jenny, who was supposed to come, just canceled. He responds that he just needs to use some drops to rid his eyes of redness, then he'd love to come. So, we go. Carina and Elise in the back and teary-eyed Erik in the front, texting with

Hazel. But Gröna Lund is closed, so we walk around the city instead. Erik, Elise, and Carina shop for summer clothes at Zara. I sit among blouses and shirts, waiting, and Erik sits down next to me with his new striped linen shirt in his hand and wonders where Carina and Elise went as he scrolls through his phone. He shows me a funny clip and when I lean in closer to see it better, he groans in agony and says that I smell so good. I feel irresistibly attractive. Poor Erik. I tell Erik about the police incident in Gotland, and he looks at me like I'm the saddest person in the whole world. Then his friends come and pick him up, and he leaves.

Two days later, I see on Instagram that he's gone to Palma to surprise Ben, who's there with Sheila celebrating his birthday. "The love of my life is having a birthday," he captures a picture of Ben in the bow of a boat they've rented with a salt-stained shirt and wind in his hair. I give it a like and add a heart emoji below the picture. Then I go to a party to celebrate Natalie's birthday.

The party is fun. I feel alive and hopeful again. I'm funny, flirtatious, slightly tipsy, and talkative. Nathan is there and unusually kind and caring. He talks to Jenny for a while, who goes home pretty soon after. The next day, she calls me in the morning and asks what my plans are for the day. I'm going to Ikea and then I have a bunch of other boring errands that I need to do before my move in a week. She says she'd like to come along, and like a protective bandage I don't yet know I need, she stays by my side all day. Back at my shared living space, she messages me and asks if she, Natalie, and Marisa can come over to my place. They arrive with a bottle of wine and a resolute demeanor. I have no idea what's going on as we sit in the living room, and they look at me intently and sympathetically. When Jenny says there's something they need to tell me, I understand everything in half a second. I press my palms to my face, pull my knees to my chest, and scream out loud. They talk, and I don't hear what they say, but I understand everything anyway. Erik has met someone else. No, no, no, no, no, I say over and over again.

We sit on the terrace, the others drink wine, and I've stopped crying, but my whole body is shaking, and I just stare out in nothingness. Mitch has also arrived, called by Natalie to bring valium. But I don't want to take them. We all sit there around the table, and I get a summary of everything they know. Apparently, Sheila had called Hazel and told her that Erik had brought a girl with him when he arrived at the boat. Hazel had told Nathan, who had told Jenny last night at Natalie's party.

"That's why I wanted to be with you today. I wanted to be close to you all the time. I didn't want to say anything, because I didn't want to see the change in you when you found out. I just wanted to be close to you," she says, and I think it's the nicest thing she's ever done for me.

I can't stop shaking. Natalie tries to get me to take a valium. I don't want to take any valium. I don't want to drink any wine. I just want to know as much as possible about what happened. She's not from Stockholm, she's a colleague in Madrid. I manage to piece together the clues that he must have met her during the time he was in Madrid. Most likely, that's why he was in Madrid. Presumably, that's where his sudden need for emotional and physical freedom came from. I send him a text message.

"I don't know what to say. But if you were concerned about not hurting me, then you have failed miserably. You have had a thousand opportunities to be honest with me in the past few weeks. Instead, I hear through the grapevine that you're going on vacation with some sort of flirt that you must have had parallel to me. I haven't been unclear about my feelings. The right thing would have been to tell me that you're also seeing other people. Not just that you don't want to define our relationship. I know we're in a fucked-up situation with our divorces, but I expected more from you."

Of course, there is no response. I follow Natalie and Mitch home to their place. I sit on their long chaise lounge and try to watch the first episode of *Chernobyl*. I think it's good, but it comes with massive anxiety, and I just want to go home. Home to my real home, not to my and Erik's made-up one. So, I do. I go home to my and Nathan's old house. Leo and Nathan are in our old bed, and I lie down on the edge next to Leo. And fall asleep.

The next day, I'm going to sign the contract for my new house. Jenny accompanies me to the real estate agent, and before we go in, she shows me a video that Sheila has posted on Instagram. It's from Palma, from the boat. Erik's new girl is standing in front of the camera dancing while Erik and Ben are lying on the deck talking. Erik laughs at something Ben says, his head is tilted back slightly, and the sleeves of his white shirt are rolled up. I quickly figure out that the video was posted after I sent the text message. Long after. How unaffected he looks. So happy and satisfied on his vacation. I go in and buy my house still with tears on my face. I have a hard time hearing what's being said. I just sit quietly and look down at the table and Jenny tells me where to sign. Then it's over, and I'm one house richer.

A few hours later, when I'm hiding against the wall in the garden and chain smoking, Erik replies that he has completely messed up, that he understands that I'm disappointed in him, and that he never wished me any harm. Period. That's all he has to say. But he says a lot more to Hazel, whom he is angry with for telling me and hurting me unnecessarily "since we had already ended it." I know he's writing this because Hazel sends me copies of their conversation while they're talking. It's fantastic that his energy goes to being angry with Hazel and not to asking me for forgiveness. That's how little I mean to him. That's how weak his feelings are. This is when I should proudly and dignifiedly just delete him from my phone and never talk to him again. But I'm so angry that he's lying, on top of everything. I send three texts in a row. I call him a fucking creep and say that Hazel sails up as a moral angel in comparison. I hope it hurts because I know how low he thinks her morals are. He just responds with another text saying that he has been clear that he didn't see us as exclusive and when he realized I didn't agree, he ended it right after he had sex with his colleague in Spain and that he doesn't know what he wants.

I reply: "Now we know at least. I never want to see you again."

Feeling satisfied with my punchy final line, I put the phone down. My whole body is shaking, but I can't even cry anymore. It's like the humiliation has completely paralyzed me. I feel worthless. Erik didn't do anything wrong. It was me who made the mistake of allowing myself to get hurt. I quickly think the thought, but it doesn't produce any emotional waves. Since everyone else thinks he did something terribly wrong, I'm swept up in the storm of opinions. It doesn't matter. Nothing matters except that I'm insignificant.

Erik is back home. He's at his and Hazel's house, arguing with Hazel. Jenny, Natalie, and I are in my garden, which soon will only be Nathan's, celebrating Natalie's birthday. Hazel calls completely panicked. Erik sent her a cryptic text saying he couldn't take it anymore and now he isn't answering his phone.

"He's so fucking broken, Ninni. I'm genuinely scared he's going to do something stupid. I don't know what to do," she says, her voice thick with tears.

I sigh. "But Hazel, of course he would never do anything. He's just tired of the fighting."

"But I've never heard him like this. I'm far from home, and Mom and Dad aren't nearby either. Ben is at work. Please, can you go and check up on him?"

Of course, I go. I tell Jenny and Natalie that I have to run a quick errand and drive over to Erik's. The door is open, and I call out without getting an answer. I go up the stairs. He's asleep in Carina's bed. I stand by the bed.

"Erik!"

He sits up groggily and stares at me with swollen eyes. His face is red from long crying. Self-pity lingers like a wet blanket over the whole room. I put my hands on my hips and tilt my head.

"What? What are you doing here?" he says, noticeably confused and a little shocked.

"What are you doing? The whole world is looking for you. Hazel thinks you've killed yourself."

He reaches for his phone.

"I couldn't take the arguing anymore," he says in a thick voice.

"Can you at least answer her, so she knows you're not dead?"

He sends a quick text and then hides under the covers and starts crying again. "I have so much fucking anxiety. The only thing I didn't want was to hurt you. I'm such a fucking idiot. There's one person in the whole world I care about besides my kids, and I screw it up for some damn junk," he sobs.

I sit on the edge of the bed. I know he's not sad for me. I know he's sad for Hazel and for the divorce and for the fact that everyone now thinks he's an asshole. He might be a little sad that he's lost his security blanket. I feel sorry for him, and we hug, but he breaks away and rushes into the bathroom to blow his nose loudly.

I walk toward the stairs, ready to leave, and he rushes to me and hangs on to me like a little monkey.

"I'm soorrry!" he cries again.

I pat him on the back. "It's okay. It will be okay."

I feel completely empty. He's so overflowing with emotions and self-pity that I can't feel anger or love. I feel in control. The ball is in my court. He regrets it, and I care.

I call Hazel from the car on the way home. "He's really broken," I say.

"I know," Hazel says worriedly. "I've never seen him like this."

"He thinks everyone hates him too. That everyone thinks everything is his fault and that he's the worst person in the world," I say.

"I don't think that," Hazel says. "He's never done anything wrong to me. I was married to him for thirteen years and he was never unfaithful. I don't know what he's doing right now."

"He seems really fragile," I say. "It's important that we talk to everyone else and make sure this backstabbing stops. People don't know everything that's happened between us, and it doesn't feel fair for him to be put in the pillory like this. I'm afraid that it will ultimately break him."

"I agree, I'll talk to everyone," Hazel says. "He's actually a very nice person who's just really struggling right now."

When I get back to Natalie and Jenny's, he sends a text thanking me. He apologizes again for hurting me and says that I mean everything to him, but that he doesn't think he can feel love. He feels empty.

I'm empty too. I reply: "You know what? It's actually okay. You and I were a bad idea from the start, and now we're going our separate ways, which is probably a good thing."

I'm lying, of course. I don't want to go our separate ways at all. I think we're a great idea. If only he could understand that we could have a fantastic life together. We're so similar in every way except the good ones right now, but that can change, I think to myself.

He just thinks I'm everything because he's lost everything else. It's easy to be someone's everything then. All I've done is keep a bed warm for him and answer the phone when he calls. He can't feel love because I'm not the kind of person he can fall in love with. The thought flutters through my brain so easily and quickly that I barely even notice it.

After a few days of sanitizing Erik's and my life together, I move back to my shared accommodation and start preparing to move out. When I return to my and Nathan's house, I find Benito, my beautiful Bengal cat, in a terrible condition. He's lying in the armchair in the bedroom and tries to get up when I come in but falls back down and croaks instead of meowing. When I pick him up, he's a tired sack of cat body in my arms. I take him to the animal hospital, and a day later, he's dead. Somewhere in the neighborhood around our house, he got hold of some glycol fluid, which he happily lapped up, and couldn't be saved. Life spins fast, faster, fastest. I am a grief that never ends. And I feel like the loneliest person in the world.

When I'm in the car, I get a text from Erik. He writes that he's heard about my cat, and he knows how much it hurts because he's had a cat himself. I reply, and we text for a while about pets.

I'm buying plants for my new house, and I call Nathan with a question about flowers when he tells me that he and Hazel are having drinks for him at our old house on his birthday. Natalie's and Jenny's families will come, as well as Hazel's and Erik's former best friends.

"I understand that it might feel a little strange in our old home and with your best friends," Nathan says quickly, "but I talked to Natalie and she said that I have to be allowed to celebrate my birthday. And they're actually my friends too. Under other circumstances, I would have wanted you to be there, too, but this year it doesn't feel right, especially not with regard to Hazel and all."

It's completely okay, I say, who of course also thinks it would have been inappropriate for me to be there, but who also doesn't really understand why Nathan absolutely has to celebrate at our house with my best friends exactly one week after I moved out.

And when we hang up, I write a long email to him explaining how coldly he's acting and how hurt I am.

Nathan doesn't reply. He's probably doing the right thing.

The weekend before, Jenny and Natalie went to Natalie's summer place for a break, and I got mad at them, too, for leaving me alone in the middle of moving and heartache. I also wrote a long email to them accusing them of abandoning me when I needed them the most.

Yes, I feel incredibly lonely, abandoned, bitter, and exposed. Nobody is there for me. My friends, especially Jenny, who are usually by my side almost every minute of my currently completely failed life, take a break in the countryside for a long weekend. But I don't give them that because I'm so busy feeling like the loneliest and most wounded person in the world.

14

REBOUND REUNION

I go home to Gothenburg. I always go back there when I feel lost and abandoned. There, they've only had me in small portions and have not yet grown tired of my way of bulldozing my life. There I get to lie on Bridget's couch, listen to music, drink wine, go for walks, get comforted, and fall asleep in front of British TV series with my mom. One evening, when I'm on my way to Bridget's for a barbecue, Erik calls. I don't answer. I can't talk to him yet. He texts and says he just wants to know how I'm doing and wonders if I need help with anything in the new house. He also writes that he has a friend who can do carpentry.

That's how it starts. Short texts that I sometimes respond to, sometimes not, and phone calls that I never answer. But I know he's on his way back in. I know that one day I will answer and everything will start again. And I hope that then everything will be different.

My surviving cat Lola is chased by one of the neighborhood's slightly meaner, larger cats. She flees up the tall plum tree right outside my window. Then she can't come down. I sit on the kitchen couch by the window and watch her, thinking that she'll eventually come down. But more and more people gather under the tree, children and adults lure and beckon to Lola to come down, but she just stares down at them in terror and climbs higher and higher up. I take Emma for a walk and Erik calls.

"I hear you have a problem with a cat," he laughs. "Should I come and get her down?"

Of course, Ben has called Erik, who's the solver of everything. People usually call him.

"No, she'll come down by herself," I say. "It's a very tall tree, impossible to climb up."

"I can get her down," he says confidently.

We continue to talk during my walk. About divorce, everyone's opinions, conflict avoidance, how Erik is doing, and how I'm doing. When I get home, one of the neighbors has pulled out a ladder, and Danny is building a contraption of a long pole, several sticks, and a basket of cat food to lure Lola down. But Lola refuses. Eventually, Erik walks along the street. He climbs up the tree, takes Lola by the scruff of the neck, and finally she's down. Noticeably traumatized, she sneaks under my stairs and stares accusingly at Erik and the rest of us.

In the evening, I go to Maya's fortieth birthday party, but I don't stay long. Instead, I text Erik. We meet at my place and drink wine. He says he's in love with me and just wants to be with me. That he hasn't been honest, either with me or himself, about how much and how strongly he really feels for me. The last thing he says before we kiss each other is "be gentle with me."

Then everything goes black. We hide at my place for three days and talk and talk . . . about everything. I dive straight back into him again without a thought of being gentle with myself.

At first, I don't dare tell anyone that Erik and I have started seeing each other again. I'm afraid that I'll see my own doubts reflected in them. And that's exactly what happens. They don't say much, but I feel it anyway. That I've made a bad choice now. That I'm choosing someone who will never be able to love me because I don't think I'm worth any better. I see my worst fears reflected in everyone I tell. But I don't say anything to Erik because when I'm with him, I don't remember them anymore. Right now, everything feels intoxicatingly good. He sees me. Right into everything that I am. There is nothing that he doesn't accept, nothing that is ugly or that I need to hide or pretend to be something that I'm not. Except that I'm five years older than him. And not nearly as beautiful as his ex-wife who is nine years younger than me, who he's still not over. He says he's over her, but not what she did to him. And when he cries over what happened, he's careful to point out that it doesn't diminish his feelings for me.

The summer is ours. When we're apart, we're still in constant contact. I feel his need for me. He wants to know where I am. What I'm doing.

How I'm feeling. I celebrate Midsummer with Natalie, Mitch, Jenny, Danny, and all the kids, and in the middle of the night when Erik calls and wakes me up, I go out in my t-shirt and walk on the wet grass and join him at his party, on his walk through the woods, when he lies in a pile of hay in some barn and has become too drunk. When the kids and I travel to Mallorca with Jenny, Danny, Mitch, and Natalie and all the kids, he wants to know what I'm doing, what I'm up to, and how I'm feeling. I feel loved and needed. It feels like he can't get enough of me. It feels like we're feeling exactly the same now. And I forget that's how it's always felt. To me.

I argue with Jenny and Natalie. The whole trip feels like there's a wall between us. Jenny says that I use my phone as a shield between them and that I'm not really present. We argue about Nathan and how I think Natalie talks to him about things she shouldn't. They say it feels unsafe to be with me now, and they never know how I'll react, how much I'll scream, and why can't I just understand that they want what's best for me. I say they should think about why I feel that way. What is it in their behavior that makes me experience it like this? We don't understand each other. We don't speak the same language anymore. It doesn't feel at all like we want what's best for each other and that the sense of security and belonging to a family is gone. When we leave Mallorca, we're less friends than before. *Do they even like me? Do I like them?* When did the sense of security and the natural belonging disappear, I don't know, but I know it's gone now.

After Mallorca, the kids go to Nathan, and I go to Gothenburg. Erik arrives and we borrow Bridget's house, travel around, visit my Gothenburg friends, and everyone thinks Erik is fantastic. Warm, soft, and heartfelt. He makes them feel so comfortable and relaxed, they say. One evening, Erik's Spanish ex-girlfriend texts him and I get angry. But it's totally okay because Erik says he understands. It's such a fundamentally different way from the way that Nathan handled me being jealous after his infidelity that I believe it means Erik is better for me in every way. Now I'm with someone who allows for all emotions, and I never have to pretend to be someone I'm not.

15

WRECKAGE

But with fall comes another change. After my biggest—and final—fight with Natalie and Jenny, I come home to an Erik who has crashed again. When I look at him and he looks at me, there's a void behind his eyes. And he never once says that he's in love with me. Once, Maya asks him straight out, and he just looks at her silently. Now, he says he just likes me a lot. I think he needs time. It took him six months to tell Hazel he loved her. Yes, he just needs time,

There's been too much of everything, and I just have to focus on myself for now while he does what he wants. We sleep together every night except when we have the kids, then we usually just have dinner together and then we go to our respective homes. It's not far since we live a block apart.

Erik's two children quickly become close to me, so very close that I can't protect myself from their love. I think they probably just miss their mom and that's why they turn to me, sometimes almost more than to Erik. But when I hold their little bodies in my lap, or when Carina lies lightly between me and Erik at night, it's hard not to accept them. I hope they are my new family. That they and my children who are already a family on Nathan's side will continue to be so. I love the chaos that ensues at dinner time when everyone is everywhere at the same time and Cole and Carina are fighting in front of the TV while Erik and I are arguing about the spot in front of the stove. We drink wine and listen to music. And everything feels like a real family. But something doesn't feel quite right. I don't know if it's me or if it's Erik or if it's both of us, but I can't stop feeling him in every minute. Does he want this? I don't know, and I never feel completely secure.

After seven months, he says he's never really felt in love with me, and he doesn't know what it means. I say, yes, but in the beginning, when he was in such a hurry to come home to me, wasn't he in love then? He says, yes, but he hasn't been able to hold onto that feeling.

We sit at my kitchen table, and Erik can't stop talking. I can't answer. I can't say anything because I can only wonder what's wrong with me. Why am I impossible to fall in love with—again. He says that he feels 95 percent, but the last 5 percent is missing, and he doesn't know what would happen if he were attracted to someone else.

I ask if we should break up, and he says he doesn't know, but maybe we should go talk to someone.

It's like he thinks this is a joint problem between us. As if I can help him fall in love with me. But all that happens is that I get frozen in the persona of someone who can't be loved. What should I do with this information?

Eventually, I start shaking. The chill rushes unabated through my body from my toes up my legs and through my whole body. I want to ask him to leave, but I don't want to be alone. I stand in the middle of the room and can't look him in the eye, I just cry and shake.

I want to go to Jenny's, who lives in the house opposite, but we don't talk anymore. I got angry with her and Natalie and said we needed a break. And when I wanted to talk a week later, they said they needed a longer break. It's been two months now. We don't even say hi anymore when we pass each other in the street, so it's a little difficult to go over to Jenny's. Erik hugs me. I can't hug back, I just stand there, shaking and crying, and let myself be held.

We go to bed, me in the fetal position and him behind me holding my trembling body tight, all night.

I wake up with a start way too early the next morning. I wriggle out of Erik's sleeping limbs that still hold me in a tight grip and go down to the bed in the basement. My body is still an insecure place, but Erik's embrace feels even worse. I need to be alone. Erik comes down as soon as he wakes up, dressed in a suit and on his way to work. He is so regretful and looks sadly at me with his head tilted.

"How are you?"

"Not so good. I don't know what to do," I answer and don't want to talk about it.

"It went really bad yesterday. I didn't mean for you to take it that way. We need to talk more later," he says.

I can't look at his sad eyes and stubbornly stare down at my clenched hands. I just want him to go.

"I'll call you later, okay?" he says and kisses me on the forehead.

When he's gone, I start crying again. I'm trapped in the feeling of panic and don't know where to go, but eventually, I also go to work.

The day is long. My body shivers constantly. I'm waiting for Erik to contact me, but also afraid he will. I don't want to talk anymore. I don't want to hear any more of his thoughts and doubts. But finally, he calls me from the tram on his way home.

"How are you?" he asks in a silky voice. "We have to talk about this. Can I come to your place?"

And I say yes, because it's probably for the best. And two hours later, we sit at the same kitchen table, on opposite sides of it, and we drink tea, not wine.

"Do you remember that story you told me about the mice and the button?" he asks.

I remember. I had heard about a project on the radio where they talked about how addiction is created. They had done an experiment with mice where researches taught the mice that if they pressed a button, they would get food. The mice quickly learned to press the button, and the food came as promised every time. But then they changed the rules, and the mice only got their reward on certain occasions when they pressed the button. Sometimes when they pressed, nothing happened. The mice went crazy. Completely obsessed, they pressed the button again and again and again. Sometimes the food came, sometimes it didn't. It seemed that the uncertainty of the reward was the trigger for their obsession.

"I wonder if I'm like the button was for those mice. That I am your button." he says and laughs a little.

What should I say to that? He's probably right. But how does that help me? What does he mean? That I should stop seeing him?

"I talked to Lucas today for a long time. And I know what that 5 percent is. It's anxiety. It's that feeling of uncertainty that I miss with you.

I don't need to chase. I don't need to wonder. I'm sure of you, completely sure. And that's very unusual for me in a relationship. That's why I think something is missing. But I don't want that kind of relationship; I want to learn how to be happy in a secure relationship."

"Well, then we know we shouldn't move in together, at least," I say.

And Erik starts crying.

"Why are you crying?" I ask.

"Well, I'm so fucked up," he says, rubbing his clenched fists against his eyes.

We talk for a long time. My joints soften more and more with each word.

"I want to be with you. You're so damn smart and wonderful, I feel good with you. And you make me very happy. You're not oversensitive," he says. "You're just emotional. And that's not wrong. You have to stop thinking it's wrong and instead embrace it."

I lower my shoulders, my breathing goes back to normal, and Erik hugs me.

"You can't pretend that you don't feel anything," says Erik. "But you have to be humble because the truth you create isn't the truth. There's another version. And instead of trying to push the feeling away, which can cause it to explode eventually, maybe you should try to ventilate it—humbly—when you have it, instead of marinating it and creating a truth out of the feeling."

I know this. I know I have a hard time distinguishing between my truth and the actual truth. And now I'm soaking up Erik's version of the truth like an alcoholic at a party.

"You're so super smart," he says. "But it's all moving too fast in your head. I love that you're emotional. You never pretend or hold anything back. But when it's thrown at me as a flurry of accusations and truths, I end up in a defensive position."

It's just so hard for me to imagine venting everything I feel, right when I feel it. The idea of letting things marinate should really be the right thing to do. The problem is that I can't relate to my thoughts rationally. I find evidence for my truth, often quite successfully. And fear and self-loathing take over. And I act impulsively. But right now, it feels warm and safe again. Everything inside that's been racing around becomes calm. And we continue.

During the sports break, we all go to Marrakesh together, with Erik's best friends Ben and Sheila and their kids. *Now we're really like a family, aren't we?* We take care of each other's children and argue over iPads and the fact that Erik and Ben want alone time. The kids have their rooms, and we have ours, and when we switch hotels, Carina sleeps between us at night. I'm starting to feel safe. Maybe it'll all work out. It almost feels real. But when we come home, I get sick. It's March and the Covid pandemic has started to take over the world. People are worried and talking ominously about death and economic collapse. I don't think about it much. But I don't see anyone because I'm in bed coughing. The kids are with Nathan and Hazel, and even though I'm sick, Erik comes and sleeps with me. The week after that, it's quiet. He doesn't call. I call, but he says he's feeling down and needs to think and be alone.

I'm going crazy waiting for the phone to ring. But I can't call him. I mustn't call. Because then I'm a bother. Because he's signaled that he wants to be left alone. Because he's not calling like he used to. My body is carbide. I can't focus on the good, like the fact that I had a very nice time with Natalie and Mitch yesterday. Natalie actually wants us to be friends again. But I keep thinking about Erik not calling. And I have to wait. Waiting is awful. Outside is "Corona" land and the world is shutting down. I think we should be able to talk to each other then. I think we should be able to behave like we're in a relationship and call each other.

On Friday, I ask if we should meet, but he's going to Ben's for dinner and doesn't ask if I want to come along. I ask him to come over to me before that so we can talk for a little while at least. When he comes, he looks sad, and I'm empty but also terrified. He says he's feeling bad and that he's so tired of not being able to get rid of all the thoughts that keep looping in his head. He kisses me on the forehead and walks away. Like a goodbye. Like a Judas kiss. Like I'm his mom who he dutifully visited in the hospital. I can't move. Sitting like a stone statue and letting his lips touch my forehead. It's almost like they're not even touching it, so cool is the kiss. He breaks up without saying anything.

Next day, I go for a walk with Maya and tell her what happened. She says what I already know: "Ninni, you have to break it off."

It's already over, but since he refuses to say it and only plans to sneak out of our relationship without explanation, it's up to me to execute it now. Maya has been skeptical of my relationship with Erik from the start. Skeptical because she sees signs of an emotionally unavailable person in a relationship with someone who desperately tries to become something he can fall in love with.

I call Bridget.

"You have to break up. Now," she says.

Bridget likes Erik because she only met him that summer in Gothenburg when we were in love and he showed a warm, caring and sociable side, which is also him.

"He needs to deal with his shit, Ninni," she says. "He's not done."

She has repeated this like a mantra from day one. But I know that if you're with the right person, you can both be done at the same time. Now I'm clinging to the hope that he might want me (again) if he thinks he's going to lose me (again). I have to dare to let go to get him.

I have to do it. So, the next day I send a text:

"Hi. I know it's low to do this via text, but I just don't have the strength to do it face to face. I can't take it anymore. I love you, and I know I should sit tight again and let you sort yourself out, but it loops. It creates too much uncertainty for me, and it won't be good in the long run either. I think we have such a fantastic time together when we're good. You give me a lot of love and warmth and security. But these moments when you become uncertain tear everything apart, especially me. I don't think you're done. And I can't wait any longer for you to be, if it's even possible while we're together. Take care of yourself and your beautiful children."

He replies that he knows. That he just needs to be completely alone. And then three hearts.

16

THE WORST IS YET TO COME

Is it all over now? It certainly seems that way. My body is reacting as though it is, with no appetite and sleeplessness. All I can do is lie in bed and watch mindless reality TV shows like *Paradise Hotel* and *Ex on the Beach*. The feeling of loneliness is consuming me, penetrating every single cell of my being.

Jenny sends me a text message saying that she's heard about Erik and that she thinks it's probably for the best. Natalie also contacts me and says that she's heard about the breakup but understands that it was my decision and is happy that I'm taking care of myself.

But was it really my decision? It doesn't feel that way at all. I can't help feeling sorry for myself, especially when I see pictures on Instagram of Natalie having a fun time with her closest friends, who aren't me.

Ben contacts me every day, and I know he's struggling with the situation as well. Erik's probably feeling sorry for himself, too, since he couldn't love me enough. I have one week to gather myself and try to cope with what's happened. The kids are coming on Friday, and I'm not sure how I'm going to hold it together when they're with me. Leo becomes very sad when I'm feeling down, and I can't take care of him in that state. He can't take care of himself either, and Nathan will be angry with me if I let my feelings affect the kids.

So, I decide to buy a cat. My other cat is with my mother, who took care of her over the school break, and the cat seems much happier there than she ever was with us. I searched online for kittens and found one that is ready to move out immediately. It's an ocicat, the same breed that Erik had before and said that he wanted again. I'm torn between the desire to buy a cat right away and the fear that others, especially Erik, will think I'm buying the cat for him. As if I could somehow lure him back by bringing his cat home.

In the end, the need for a cat wins, and when the kids arrive, we drive to Uppsala to pick up Elin, the kitten. Elin turns out to be a real charmer, a bit sad at first, but then she curls up on my chest and looks at me with her yellow-brown eyes, as if to say everything will be okay. She plays fetch with me, dropping the ball into my lap so I can throw it again.

I tell the kids about the breakup with Erik, and they seem to take it well. They say that he wasn't nice, and there's no major drama. They still have their stepsiblings, and the only thing they've lost is Erik, who used to play Leo's sensitive songs at full volume, even though he knew it made Leo cry every time. When the kids fall asleep, I lie in bed and cry myself to sleep in front of *Paradise Hotel*.

After the weekend, when the kids have gone to school, I can't find Elin. Panic sets in as I think Elise may have left the door open, allowing Elin to escape. I have lost all the cats I've ever had. I gave away my first cat Alice during Nathan and my first crisis because Nathan couldn't handle her anymore. Despite my efforts to make life bearable for Nathan, I agreed to let her go, which was tough on the kids. Now, they don't even remember Alice.

A year after Alice, we bought Johnny Olsson from my sister. He was a very affectionate cat who preferred everyone else but us. I had to pick him up at the clothing store on the square, at Elise's classmate's mother's house, and another family's home a few blocks away. Eventually, my sister insisted that he be allowed to come home again, as he clearly did not want to live with us. After that, we were without a cat for a while.

During the year when Nathan and I tried living apart, and I was preparing to live alone, I bought two Bengal cats, two sisters named Lola and Pixie. Lola was not particularly fond of us, but Pixie was affectionate, playful, and quite amazing. One night, we found her strangled by a thread hanging from a curtain. She had played with the thread, and it had wrapped around her neck like a noose. Her fur was all matted from Lola's tongue, who tried to lick her back to life during the night. Three months later, we bought Benito. He drank poison and died last year, just after Nathan and I separated.

All of these cat lives, and how each death was somehow my fault, races through my mind as I walk around the neighborhood calling for Elin. I cry so much that I can barely catch my breath. Eventually, I start hyperventilating and call Ben for help. He comes out to search for the cat. I call Jenny and Danny, who help me print out fliers. While standing in the garden crying and smoking, Erik suddenly appears on the path outside. He tilts his head and asks how I'm doing.

"Not so good," I say and when he hugs me, I cry even more. We go inside and have coffee. Erik wants to talk, and I'm afraid he wants to talk about us, so I talk about everything else. We go outside again to look for Elin, but she is nowhere to be found.

A few hours later, I find her in a box under Leo's bed, and I feel ashamed. The next morning, Erik comes by to check if I'm okay, and I go with him to have coffee with Ben. When we arrive, Ben is quite surprised and asks what was going on.

"Are you two together again?" he wonders.

"No, we're just fuck buddies," I reply. "We had sex just before we came here."

It's not particularly funny, but everyone laughs with relief.

It's only been a week since Erik and I broke up, and it's clear that we can't start hanging out as friends yet. But we keep running into each other wherever we go. He lives just a few houses down, and his best friend lives across from me, so it's hard to avoid each other. One afternoon when I meet Ben, I can't help but cry. Ben becomes a bit uncomfortable, but he comforts me as best he can. An hour later, Erik knocks on my door. He rushes in and hugs me, asking how I'm doing. I cry big black splotches on his yellow vest.

"I just feel so incredibly alone," I sniffle.

"I know," he says. "I was thinking about it yesterday. It's so terrible not to be anyone's person anymore. I'm so unused to being alone, and not having anyone is scary."

That's a strange statement from Erik, "Anyone's person." He's sad because he's not someone's person. I think he's Ben's person, but I don't say anything.

Before Erik and I broke up, I started going to Sabrina, a hypnotherapist in Uppsala. She is particularly focused on highly sensitive personality types and talks about me as if I am also highly sensitive. I've always thought of it as a bit like an allergy to electricity. When Elise was a baby, I stumbled upon the concept of HSP—Hyper Sensitive Personality—and thought maybe she was one. She always wanted to be close, so I carried her in a baby carrier until she was two, among other things. But I've always dismissed the idea that I might be one because there's so much that doesn't fit.

She described an HSP personality as: *Prefers to stand on the sidelines rather than jump right into a new social situation in order to have time to observe and reflect before actively engaging.*

Hardly. It's my first thought. I throw myself headlong into every situation, strip naked, and speak out about everything I'm thinking in the same moment I'm thinking it. But that can really vary. And it's probably only in recent years that that behavior has dominated. But I'm impulsive, always. I never think things through—I just go with my gut.

Is very aware of details, nuances, and small contrasts.

God, no. I see the big picture. I'm terrible with details. But do they mean details in a specific situation, in a social situation? If so, then yes. There are probably a few things I miss.

Wants to consider all the details and possible consequences before acting. This means that as an HSP, one often makes decisions more slowly than many others.

No, no, no, never.

Is more aware of other people's thoughts and feelings than most people are because they are good at capturing and interpreting social nonverbal signals.

Definitely yes. But I've always thought that it's a result of my mom never saying what she really thought or felt, so I had to figure it out for myself so I could act accordingly. That has created a pattern of always sensing what everyone else is thinking so I can adapt to what they want. And all those other gut feelings about what people are thinking are usually just based on my own flaws and insecurities.

Acts more conscientiously than others because they are strongly focused on cause and effect.

Maybe. But isn't that also based on the fear of not being loved if I don't act conscientiously?

Is unusually concerned about social injustices and the environment, and often expresses strong emotional engagement.

No. I only care about humans. And animals. I don't even sort my trash.

Gifted, artistic, or passionate about various art forms.

Definitely not.

Often describes a greater emotional reaction than others in various situations.

It's hard to deny. Throughout my life, I've consistently been told that I'm oversensitive, overreactive, and so on. I think it's because I've often chosen to be close to people who aren't particularly sensitive.

Believes that nature has a particularly healing and calming effect, or is more moved by its beauty than others. Enjoys animals, plants, and being near or in water.

Completely agree.

Often has unusually vivid or colorful dreams.

It's hard to say since I only have my own to compare to, but yes.

Sabrina goes so far as to say that my mother is likely hypersensitive too. Yes, she is certainly sensitive. But all her feelings are locked deep inside and mainly manifest through headaches, joint pain, and stomach problems. Strong emotions have always been scary for Mom, and also for me. I've always thought it was because of my need for control, but the more I talk to Sabrina, the more I wonder. Perhaps my need for control comes from an unusually strong register of emotional reactions that I haven't known how to handle. It's hard to know what's what.

Anyway, I'm sitting with Sabrina again. We always talk for a while first, then she hypnotizes me, and with her intuition, she can follow what I see when I see it. Even though I'm skeptical, I always feel really good after a visit, and this time is no exception. After she counts down, she asks me to see my inner core in front of me. A core in transformation. It's enclosed in a cocoon. Sabrina asks if there's a butterfly waiting inside. But the butterfly isn't soft and delicate; its wings are large and heavy with scales. When it breaks free from the cocoon and soars into the air with mighty, powerful wings, Sabrina wonders if it's really a butterfly.

"No, it's a dragon," I say. The dragon sweeps high over, watching over me in times when I need it most.

When I get home, I Google dragons as power animals—there's been a lot of talk about power animals from Natalie and Jenny lately, probably from one of their new friends who has inspired them. Everyone wants to find their inner power animal. When I read about dragons, I see that they are a power animal that signals change, transformation, and finding one's spiritual side.

It's getting more and more like spring outside. I spend a little more time with Natalie, Jenny, Marisa, and their new friends. When they go to eat lunch at the restaurant down the street, Jenny asks if I want to come along. The seat across from me is empty, and when a woman I've never met before comes in a little while after everyone else, she ends up sitting next to me. Her name is Alexis, and she just separated from Hazel's first boyfriend, Elijah. She says she's afraid of being alone. I find her quite uninteresting, but I listen politely and answer her questions about how I've been dealing with my grief.

"It's a process that you have to give time," she says. "I've been really sad, but I'm doing well now."

"What have you done then?" I ask.

"I've meditated," she replies shortly.

I have never been able to meditate, and I think I'm further from it than ever now when all I want to do is cry in front of TV reality shows.

When I get home, I message Erik that I just met Alexis and that he should date her. He puts a question mark on the message, and I reply that it would be a perfect closed circle if he got together with Hazel's ex-boyfriend's ex-wife. He doesn't respond.

A few weeks later, I'm at dinner with Ben and Sheila, and Ben tells me that Erik has started going to Reiki healing with Alexis. Alexis is nine years younger than me, the same age as Hazel. She is cool and reserved and perfectly feminine. The only thing preventing Erik from wanting her is her profession. Erik, who just days before we broke up, got a large light bulb tattoo on his shoulder with "Don't feel—think" is very hostile toward anything spiritual. If he can be open to it by going to Reiki healing himself, there is nothing stopping him from falling in love with Alexis. All of these calculated risks quickly run through my mind as I tell Ben that they will get together. Ben laughs and says that Erik is still very far from being with anyone. He is still licking his wounds. But I can't let it go, and when I meet Alexis for lunch at Marisa's house a few days later, I feel an instinctive jealousy. I know it is baseless, and when Alexis and I stand in the kitchen loading the dishwasher, I decide to be honest with her so she can understand why I am so hesitant. I immediately start crying.

"Come on, let's go in here," says Alexis, leading me into another room.

I'm crying uncontrollably now and saying that I'm just so tired of him showing up in every situation.

"I don't know Erik, I just treat him. We don't talk," says Alexis. "But Ninni, I'm closed off. And I didn't think you were still in love with him."

"Yes, I'm deeply in love with him," I cry. "I'm waiting for him to decide. Everything ended so suddenly and without any real explanation."

"It's so sad when two people aren't right for each other," says Alexis warmly, patting me on the back. Then she smiles broadly. "Everything will be fine."

"Can you at least promise me to tell me if anything happens between you two?" I ask.

She looks me straight in the eye. "I promise to tell you if anything happens," she says.

She ends the conversation by telling me I shouldn't drink so much.

When Alexis has left, the part about her and Erik still gnaws at me. "Why didn't she just say that there absolutely won't be anything?" I vent to everyone still sitting at the table, including Alexis's best friend Norah.

"Oh, that's just Reiki talk, probably," says Marisa. "Erik is so far from what Alexis is looking for."

"I know the jealousy is completely irrational, that's why I felt safe venting it to her," I say.

"Well, of course you're jealous," says Norah. "All guys fall for her. I mean, look at her. She's gorgeous."

I don't think she's particularly gorgeous, but I guess Erik does, and I know he wants to be with someone who everyone else sees as a catch.

Alexis texts me later in the evening and asks how I am doing. I say that I'm okay, but that I'm so tired of never getting over him and him showing up in every situation. Even among these girlfriends whose company I've just started to appreciate. She tells me that I'm beautiful and too hard on myself.

I don't understand what she means. How am I being hard on myself? I'm just sad.

17

CTRL ALT DELETE

A couple of weeks later, I'm sitting with my friend Sara drinking wine. We drink a lot of wine, and when I'm a bit too drunk to function, I decide to go to Erik's place to pick up all my stuff that's still there. Maybe it's time for us to talk as well. It's been so long, and he says he's doing better. But he's not home. I text him, and he tells me he's at Ben's and asks me to come over. I hesitate. I know it's a bad idea. Everything is a bad idea. I call Bridget and promise her that I'll go home while I continue walking toward Ben's house. I'm really not sober. This is a terrible idea. Erik, Ben, and two other friends of theirs are sitting on the terrace, listening to music from Erik's phone. It rings, and when Erik answers, the sound of the call goes through the speakers. I can hear that it's a girl. Erik is gone for a long time. I'm inside the kitchen, talking to Ben when he comes back and tells me it was his brother's wife who called. The rest of the evening is quite chaotic. I'm drunk and very unpleasant to Erik, and I try to flirt with another guy who's there. When the evening is over, Erik gives me a ride home on his bike, and I think we're going to my place to have sex and then everything will be okay again. He's ready for a real relationship. With me. But when we stop outside my place, he gets ready to leave. I hug him, and we stand nose to nose when I ask him to come in for a while. He says no. But I push him into my house. When we finally get inside, I'm so drunk that I can't sit down. Instead, I lean against the kitchen counter and say that I have to have sex, that it's been too long, and that I can't have sex with someone I don't know, so it has to be with him. Erik says it's a bad idea, and I shout at him with a raised voice that he might as well go home then. Before he leaves, he stops and looks at me.

"Bye."

"Now at least you know what you want," I scream.

"No, Ninni," he says with a tired voice. "I don't."

I stumble into bed and text him that he's an idiot and that I never want to talk to him again.

But the next day, I realize that it's probably exactly what I have to do. I have to have a confirmed ending. All these flirty encounters on the street, all the unclear messages about where he is, what he wants, and above all, how we stopped seeing each other in March, make it hard to move on. I'm still waiting for him. I text him: "I regret it. I do want to meet. Can we talk?"

He replies, absolutely, and a few hours later, he knocks on the door. I suggest a walk, and we head out onto the street. It's so warm. I wave to Norah across the street, who's out walking her dog.

"I'm sorry for yesterday," I say as we start walking.

"Yeah, you pulled a real #MeToo on me," he laughs.

I don't laugh. We walk down to the meadow and the water.

"How are you doing now?" I finally say.

"Well, actually pretty good. I've landed—in everything," he says with emphasis on everything.

"And what have you landed in then?"

He's quiet for a moment. "That you and I are over."

There it was. My ending. Now I know. Ouch.

"You could have called me and told me."

"But you said you didn't want to hear from me," he protests.

"I said I couldn't handle hanging out as friends so soon after."

"Well, I've probably done a lot of things wrong."

"I don't know what I thought. You warned me. You kept saying you weren't in love with me," I say almost to myself.

He looks down at the meadow. "I wanted to, I tried, but it didn't work out."

Ouch.

We walk down to the water, and I stop.

"Do you want to go into the woods?" he asks.

"No, I just want to go home now. That's all I wanted to hear."

"Okay," says Erik and we turn around, me a few steps ahead of him.

"Another thing," he says behind me. "Something that has nothing to do with this, but I thought you should hear it from me. I went on a date with Alexis on Monday."

Of course he did.

"Okay, I just wish she had said something. She promised she would," I say.

We stop outside his door. A couple Erik and Hazel used to hang out with pass by with a stroller on the other side of the street. He waves to them cheerfully.

"Okay, bye," I say shortly.

"Bye," he says just as shortly.

I turn and start walking quickly up the street to my house. It feels like he's still standing there looking after me, but why would he? I mean nothing to him.

For the first hours afterward, it's silent inside. No more questions left. But with the evening comes the crying, and it doesn't stop. I feel skinless, wide open, without protection. I received healing from my hypnotherapist Sabrina a few weeks ago and all I want now is to get it again. To be wrapped in a warm, soft layer of protection, because I can't handle feeling this much right now. I'm falling apart. But it's Saturday and I can't call Sabrina. So I call Madeline, a medium that Sara had recommended to me the night before. I walk on the crackling gravel path behind the terraced houses when Madeline answers. Through the tears, I manage to tell her what happened and that I need help.

"The worst part is that I don't understand how I could fool myself like that. How could I think that he felt something when he didn't?"

"You felt so strongly for him that you mixed your feelings with his, it happens sometimes," explains Madeline.

Well, that makes it feel even worse. Not only was I not clear enough to see his feelings, but apparently I even projected my own to him. I deceived both of us for a while. Everything, absolutely everything, is my fault. I cry nonstop, and Madeline promises to see me the next day.

"Do you have any angels that you can ask to be with you tonight?" she asks.

I don't have any, and Madeline says she will ask her angels to be with me during the evening.

"You will feel calm and safe already in a few hours," she assures me.

There's something about her that doesn't feel good. Through all my grief, all my tears, I still perceive her as dishonest. Her voice is high-pitched, and she speaks with a distinctive accent that grates on my ears. We end the call, but I cancel the appointment with her a few hours later. It doesn't feel safe. And when Marisa tells me a few weeks later that Madeline is one of Alexis's mentors and best friends, I understand why.

I go to work the next day. With three valiums in my body. The first time I took a valium I had to lie down on the couch because the substance weighed down my body so much that I couldn't stand. Now I'm so full of adrenaline and lack of sleep that I don't even feel them. But they keep me from breaking down in the open office landscape. Another Monday, another Monday meeting when I cry. My colleagues are so used to my constant emotional outbursts that they barely raise an eyebrow anymore. I go to work. Go home. Talk to Bridget. Text with her and Jade. They are my anchor in this. They are in Gothenburg, but closer than anyone else. I go swimming with Natalie. Lie on the dock and look up at a provocatively blue sky while Natalie offers her comfort.

"Well, that was a damn twist," she says. "I don't know Alexis very well, but she's very introverted. I think she'll get tired of Erik pretty quickly."

"But Erik is actually very spiritual, I mean, he's just what Alexis needs. And he probably reminds her of her ex-husband and someone she can save. Plus, she's young and beautiful, everything I'm not," I wail.

Natalie is silent.

"I just think it's so damn difficult to be in a relationship while processing someone else," I say helplessly, hoping she'll agree.

She doesn't.

"Well, he'll probably get over it at the same time they're together. That's usually how it goes."

Except with me, that is. Because I am someone that men can't fall in love with. I am someone that men like. As a friend. But not as a partner. I am unattractive. I am un-womanly. I am delightful and easygoing and compliant. Not an exciting, beautiful challenge that they want to conquer. But Alexis also seems delightful and easygoing. How does that fit? I constantly wonder what Alexis has that I don't. Yes, she's young. I'm old. She's beautiful. She is . . . what else is she? Maybe that's enough. I scroll through her Instagram in search of the mystery of what's wrong with me.

"Anger will come soon," says Bridget. "First sorrow, then anger, then neutrality."

But where will I find the anger? How can I be angry at someone for not being able to fall in love with me? It's not his fault, it's mine. He tried, but it didn't work. I send a text message to Erik.

"Hey. This wasn't how I thought it would be. I thought if I gave you some space, you would realize that you wanted to be with me. Now you're in love with someone else instead. Right now, I'm pretty broken, but I want you to know that I'm not angry with you at all. Instead, I hope that you can start feeling good now. You are such a wonderful person and truly deserve a lovely life full of love and joy. Take care of yourself and your beautiful children. Please don't respond to this."

He responds with a heart emoji. I wish he had answered anyway. Even if he doesn't have anything to say that I want to hear. I don't want to hear any more about how he wishes he hadn't hurt me, how he tried to fall in love with me, but he couldn't. I don't want to hear that he cares about me. It just makes me feel even more impossible to love.

18

FROM NOW ON, NOTHING CAN GO WRONG

Grief is a black hole that never ends. It's scorching hot outside, and I'm too afraid to even go out to my backyard for fear of running into someone. Ben and Sheila reach out to me regularly. Nathan and Hazel invite me to their home for Midsummer. I see on Instagram that Natalie is having dinner with her closest friends, including Alexis. I talk to Maya. I text with Bridget and Jade. I can't possibly talk to my mom because I know my grief is too much for her to handle. Just like my dad. He calls and talks about other things. I avoid my kids as much as I can because I'm afraid of scaring them with my bottomless grief and self-pity. I have no one. I must have something. A hope for something else. I must have a fantasy I can lean on. I ask Lauren to recommend a medium. I know she's been to a few. She gives me the number for a woman named Charlotte who lives in South Africa. We meet on Skype. She doesn't want to see my picture and neither do I want to see hers. So, I only hear her voice. She talks fast and enthusiastically. I will learn quickly, she says. I will write books. I will make friends again. A whole new world will open up to me. I will meet a man soon, next year even. A man who has a teenage daughter whom I've known in a past life.

Loose fantasies about things that will never come true, I think.

"Did he ever love me?" I wonder instead.

"Honey, he doesn't know what love is," she says.

I cry. I say I'm broken.

"You are not broken. This is all for the better good," she says.

She says the same thing as everyone else. And I don't understand why she's talking about my career. Or what she thinks I'm going to learn.

Lauren texts and suggests meditation at the EQ Gym. She's been doing it regularly since she started working with them. I've never meditated, and I can't imagine lying down and trying to think of nothing right now. But I try one of their free meditations via Zoom. The woman who will lead the meditation is named April. She's very pretty. Too pretty to know anything about human pain, I think as I lie in bed with my computer on my lap.

"Hello and welcome," she says cheerfully from the screen.

It's only her camera that's on. We others only show our names, like a frame around her face.

"Now we're going to do an active transcendental meditation," she says peppy. "For those of you who don't know, we start by me guiding you to a form of self-hypnosis, and then we continue on our own with an intense breathing that will take you to a theta mode where you can release your ego."

I don't understand. What is my ego? What is theta? It sounds terribly difficult to have to breathe in the way she describes. In and out through the mouth in quick, short intervals. But I do as she says.

"Now, focus all your attention on your eyelids," she says with a soft voice. "Look up. Look down. With your eyes closed."

I get dizzy.

"Now, imagine you're standing in front of a staircase, a staircase that will take you down to your inner self. Now let go of all control. From now on, nothing can go wrong."

The music is intense, and it's pushing on my breathing. I breathe quickly to the beat of the music and April's own breathing. After a while, I don't even know if I'm breathing or not, but it's no longer dark behind my eyelids. I am sitting on an earthy, dry floor. Am I in a cave? Alexis, Hazel, and Natalie's new best friend Lynne dance around me, hand in hand. Jealousy wells up from deep within, and I realize that I am jealous of all three of them. Hazel, because she is living my old life, Lynne, because she took my best friend, and Alexis, because she took my new love.

April encourages us to fill up with positive emotions.

"See yourself in front of you, like a reflection," she says.

I stare at the darkness behind my eyelids, but I can't see anything.

After a while, I see the contours of something dark and rough. It's me, but I've burned up. All that's left is charcoal. Shriveled, shrunk, and charred.

I love the meditations. Each session is like a colonic for the soul. All the emotions come at once. I sob, laugh, scream, sing, dance, run—mostly inside my body, but sometimes outside. Above all, I cry. I cry so much that I have trouble breathing and need to pause to blow my nose. All the suppressed emotions from the past years erupt like a volcano of tears.

The next morning, I wake up with a sinus infection. It aches and presses under my eyes and around my nose. I go to Marisa's and have coffee with her and her sister Isla. Afraid to say too much. Afraid to speak ill of Alexis. Afraid that they will feel sorry for me.

I haven't been sad about Erik since Saturday. No pressure on my chest. No blood vanishing from my head at the thought of him and Alexis. Oh well. They are a couple. He's in love with her. Maybe they'll be together forever. It feels okay. I see him in front of his little house by the road and how he's pottering around in his idyllic garden, grilling with Alexis and his children and her children. To say that I feel happy for him might be pushing it. But I feel warm in my body at the thought that he's happy. I think he deserves to feel good. I think it's easier to think that when I don't feel sorry for myself for not being with him.

But of course, I talk too much at Marisa's house. She and her sister tilt their heads and ask how I'm feeling with a caring tone. But I don't feel cared for; I feel like a failure because they feel sorry for me. So instead of answering how I feel, I say something about Natalie that I regret and call Alexis a spiritual influencer and declare that Erik has only found a meta-version of Hazel. I instinctively notice that they think I'm unfair, but that I can't be blamed because I'm grieving. And my contempt for myself is reflected in them.

"Alexis says she doesn't care what anyone else thinks because she can see his soul," Marisa says. "And that they probably knew each other in a past life, and that's why things have gone so quickly."

I am burning up inside. Of course Alexis can see Erik's soul. I could, too, but none of my friends could accept him because I was not credible in my judgment of him. Alexis, who has become all my old friends' spiritual adviser in a matter of months, that's something else. Erik can be in love with her. They can buy that, because it is more likely that he is in love with her than with me. She is worthy. Not me. She is lovable. Not me.

When I leave, I feel anxious. Everything I said is spinning in my head. I want to send a text and apologize, but I don't because I think it's my need for control that is pushing me to do it. I think that in my memory I said more than I actually did. Seemed less bitter than I felt I sounded. But I wish I could have refrained from speaking ill of Natalie, Jenny, and Alexis. I only remember the bad things I said about them, not the good. But saying something bad, even if it was based on my feelings, doesn't feel good. They seemed to understand me. They said they understood me. I try to tell myself that they were telling the truth. They showed empathy and concern. But I am unable to understand myself, empathize with myself, or accept that I did that. Instead, the feeling of losing control of what I said lingers in me. I think that the next time we meet, I will redo, do it right, do it better. Keep control.

19

THE BEGINNING

Because the meditations with April are so incredibly liberating, I book a one-hour coaching session with her. I'm skeptical of the word "coach" and think it means that someone is going to pep-rally me. But through the Zoom window, I've gained confidence in April and want more. We meet on Zoom as usual because April lives in LA. I hastily summarize, of course while crying, what I need help with. That I've divorced my husband, left my home, my friends, and now also my new love, and that I feel completely alone and exposed. I panic a little from my self-pitying account and am surprised that April actually seems moved by my banal story. *Love and friend drama—she must have heard worse than that, right?*

She says that the sorrow I feel now is reasonable, but that it should pass relatively quickly, otherwise it's likely old grief that has resurfaced. That has been lying dormant for a long time and has now been awakened by the new grief. I'm not entirely sure what she means. Have I had grief before? Yes, maybe, but I felt it so intensely that I find it hard to believe I wouldn't have felt it fully then. We talk for a long time, and it actually feels better than with any other therapist I've ever had. Maybe it's because I'm in the midst of grief and can more easily access my emotions. Maybe it's the meditations I'm doing in parallel. I don't know which it is, but it doesn't matter. Because I feel it beginning to ease. How the world doesn't feel as heavy anymore and how small rays of light are coming in through the darkness under my duvet.

A month later, I think I'm over him. I play "Summer Sun" by Texas on repeat and marvel at how quickly it went. And I think I'm done and that it's over, completely unaware that it has just begun.

PART 2
THE EXPANSION

WHO IS MY MIRROR?

She was an engaging, talkative, curious, and an interesting individual, making it effortless for others to like her. One could easily describe her as being quite social. At times, it was hard to understand where she was headed or what she truly meant. Nevertheless, she had a way of making everything she said ironic, funny, and lighthearted, even when sharing her darkest stories. One would say she was thoroughly entertaining. Getting to know her was a joy, as she was someone you wanted to listen to, share a cup of coffee with, collaborate on a project, and have in your life.

Her story touched me in a way that turned my stomach inside out, and while listening, I felt both grateful it wasn't me going through it and empathetic toward her. I truly liked her, even though I saw a teenager trapped inside a grown-up body.

She was an excellent communicator on the outside, but the complete opposite on the inside. It was like she was an open book, yet a closed chapter at the same time.

Today, she is my friend and cowriter for this book. I'm April, the coach. I will guide you through the general understanding of shadow work. I will help you see your triggers, your defense and coping mechanisms, your programmed beliefs, and your survival strategies.

She is Ninni, but she is also me. And maybe she is you too.

The return

The emotional pain that consumed Ninni did not come from Erik, Nathan, Alexis, Natalie, or anyone else for that matter. They were merely the catalysts that opened the doors to her suppressed and unfelt emotions and fears. Their presence—and absence—triggered a tsunami of emotions that she had buried deep beneath the surface.

As she took the plunge into the depths of her emotions, she found herself swimming in a sea of feelings that she had never allowed herself to feel before. It was overwhelming, and at times, it seemed as though she was drowning in a vortex of pain and despair. But it opened her up to the opportunity to dig deep into herself and her past.

She realized that the people in her life, like Nathan, Erik, and Alexis, all had their own issues and shadow aspects that they needed to work through. But that was not her concern. What mattered was her own story and her own healing, and that's where she needed to focus her energy.

It's not easy to face the darkest parts of ourselves, to confront our fears, insecurities, and pain. It takes a tremendous amount of courage to acknowledge our vulnerabilities and weaknesses, to open ourselves up to the possibility of healing and growth. But I knew that we had to start from the beginning, to take the first step in a long and challenging journey.

The journey ahead of her was uncertain and daunting, but she seemed determined to see it through. I knew that it would require patience, resilience, and a willingness to embrace the discomfort that comes with growth. But if she was ready to face the pain, to explore the depths of her emotions, she would emerge from the other side a stronger and more whole person.

So, together we took a deep breath, closed our eyes, and dove into the unknown. This is what we found, what we learned, and what we gained.

THE EQ GYM

The Power of Emotional Intelligence

We all inevitably experience pain in our lives, often without realizing that we are unconsciously contributing to it. Becoming aware of this truth is the journey of self-discovery.

I invite you to join us on the next step of Ninni's journey, with the hope that it will also be your own.

We'll dive deep into the shadows, exploring the wounds, triggers, behaviors, coping mechanisms, defense mechanisms, and survival strategies that have been ingrained in Ninni over the years. But this isn't a journey of blame or victimhood. No, it's a journey of taking full responsibility and accountability for our own well-being. This is a journey of transformation and growth, a journey of shedding old patterns and beliefs, and stepping into a new way of being. It won't be easy, but it will be worth it.

We all have the capability to shift our energy, going beyond the borders and limitations of being human—expanding beyond our wildest dreams if we allow ourselves to. **The EQ Gym approach comes full circle, leading us back to our roots, the wounds created in childhood, and the programming we all have. It urges us to return and examine these aspects from a different perspective, reprogramming ourselves, and sometimes even reparenting ourselves.**

Together, we'll venture into some dark places from Ninni's childhood. We'll also explore other examples that you might be able to relate to, helping you to gain a deeper understanding of yourself, and starting to unpack what no longer serves you.

The cognitive invitation

This part of the book will provide you with the tools to discover the reasons behind your actions and reactions and gain a deeper understanding of your unconscious patterns. This will help you to identify your traumas and coming out the other side more self-aware and conscious.

The brain is often referred to in terms of left and right sides. Simply put, the left side deals with logic, while the right side deals with emotions. By delving into the right side of the brain, you will uncover new facets of yourself and gain a deeper understanding of the person you are—and the person you want to be.

What is shadow work?

Shadow work is a crucial aspect of personal growth and well-being. It involves confronting and accepting the facets of ourselves that we have hidden away or rejected. All these parts are stored within us, creating a shadow self that subconsciously affects our behavior.

By getting to know our shadow, we often come to realize that the traits we dislike most in others are often a reflection of the disowned parts of ourselves. It's an eye-opening experience to see how the negative emotions that society teaches us to suppress—such as anger, sadness, shame, and fear—can actually lead to more distress when ignored.

Shadow work will help you shine a light on your unconscious and become more aware of your patterns and triggers. It's not an easy journey—it's complex—but the rewards of a stronger sense of self are well worth it. Let me show you how we did it with Ninni as inspiration for you to confront your own shadows.

SHADOW

What is blind to you but visible to others?

WHAT IS BLIND TO YOU?

*Tired, Unstable, Restless, Lethargic,
Guilt, Indifferent, Distant, Shy,
Betrayed, Insecure, Anxious,
Regretful, Unimportant, Stressed,
Worried, Isolated,
Catastrophizing, Worthless,
People-pleasing, Rejected,
Defeated, Outcast, Numb,
Validation-seeking, Shaming,
Jealous, Downcast,
Submissive, Self-critical,
Embarrassed,
Inadequate, Avoidant,
Self-loathing,
Passive,
Dismissive,
Self-medicating,
Small, Threatened,
Empty, Tense, Upset,
Irritated, Inferior, Aggressive,
Envious, Self-destructive, Paralyzed,
Ruminating, Apathetic,
Passive-aggressive, Power-abusive,
Cynical, Sarcastic, Powerless,
Judging, Victim Mentality,
Humiliated, Resentful, Indecisive,
Dominant, Self-diminishing,
Threatening, Denial*

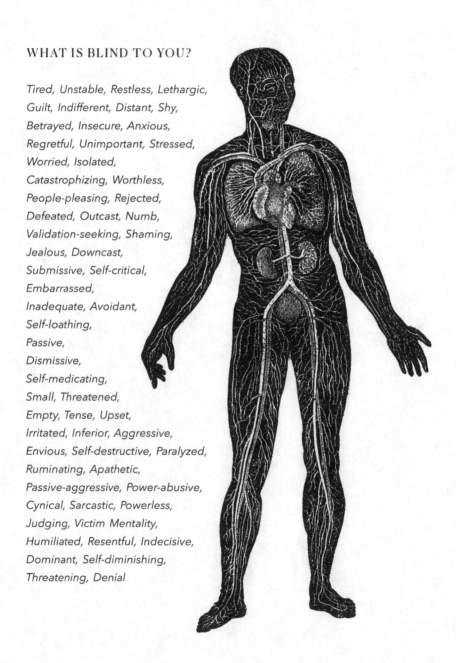

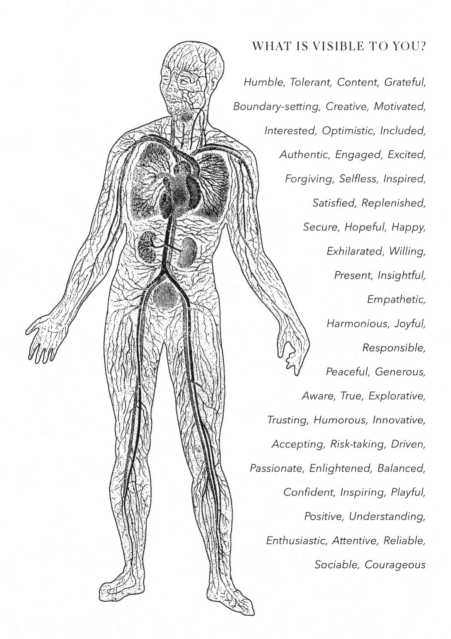

WHAT IS VISIBLE TO YOU?

Humble, Tolerant, Content, Grateful,
Boundary-setting, Creative, Motivated,
Interested, Optimistic, Included,
Authentic, Engaged, Excited,
Forgiving, Selfless, Inspired,
Satisfied, Replenished,
Secure, Hopeful, Happy,
Exhilarated, Willing,
Present, Insightful,
Empathetic,
Harmonious, Joyful,
Responsible,
Peaceful, Generous,
Aware, True, Explorative,
Trusting, Humorous, Innovative,
Accepting, Risk-taking, Driven,
Passionate, Enlightened, Balanced,
Confident, Inspiring, Playful,
Positive, Understanding,
Enthusiastic, Attentive, Reliable,
Sociable, Courageous

1

WOUNDS

The birthplace of programmed beliefs

The first eight years of a child's life are incredibly impactful in determining the type of person they become. The events that take place during this development shape us, both physically and emotionally. Our perspectives on life, others, and ourselves are programmed in the subconscious mind during these formative years. At this stage, we lack rational thinking and unconsciously associate all events around us with ourselves and our self-worth. Simply put, if our parents' divorce, we may easily believe it is our fault. If Dad leaves, it's because I'm not worthy of love. If Mom is angry, I must have done something wrong. In personal development, events that cause these associations are referred to as traumas due to the impact they have on us. We develop emotions, thoughts, perspectives, and behaviors linked to the traumatic event.

The term "trauma" within self-development should not be mistaken for the medical term trauma, which refers to a psychological lock caused by a shock-like experience leading to severe post-traumatic stress disorder (PTSD). That term usually applies to events such as war, rape, assault, death, and so on.

Within self-development, we speak of emotional PTSD, also known as complex post-traumatic stress disorder (C-PTSD). It can occur after a person has experienced prolonged and repeated trauma, such as being in an abusive relationship or being subjected to gaslighting and manipulation over an extended period of time. This type of trauma can lead to a heightened sensitivity to triggers, causing strong reactions such as panic and anxiety. However, when it occurs in our childhood, it could be something as minor as being abandoned by a best friend in preschool. If we—or life—continue to confirm these negative perspectives on ourselves when similar experiences occur, our shadow grows.

All related events linked to a trauma can create triggers. By going back in time and looking at how we perceived an event as a child, we can better understand how experiences that seem trivial to us today may have actually created a trauma—and why we are being triggered. A seemingly insignificant childhood event can create truths about ourselves that we carry with us throughout our lives, particularly in our relationships. Every time someone's actions remind us of the old trauma, we react with the same emotions as then. We get triggered—and our inner child takes over.

For example, imagine you are an infant sleeping in a stroller. Suddenly, a dog starts barking and you wake up scared and start crying. It's possible that you experience a feeling of total powerlessness for the first time. As you grow up, your body stiffens every time you see a dog. You know dogs are not dangerous, but it's hard for you to relax around them. You're unaware where your fear of dogs comes from, but it's highly noticeable. This fear of dogs is a perspective and memory stored in your subconscious.

You may also have a subconscious perspective on powerlessness. You may unconsciously live your life to avoid feeling powerless again. From a small incident that seems minor, a trauma is created. We often have no idea why we feel and behave the way we do. We no longer hear our thoughts; they operate from our subconscious as a belief and run on autopilot.

Another example could be a person who grew up in a household with a lot of anger and verbal abuse. This person may have a deep-seated belief that they are not worthy of love and constantly attract toxic relationships, as their perspective on relationships was formed by the traumatic events of their childhood. By understanding the root cause of these beliefs and behaviors, they can work toward healing and breaking the cycle.

Next, we'll examine specific scenarios and painful memories from Ninni and other clients (whose names have been changed) and explain how those traumas impacted their relationships.

Ninni's story

The wound and the programming

"I am worthless—that's why I get abandoned."
Growing up, I often felt worthless. I remember my first day at preschool. I was scared because I didn't know a single person and was clinging close to my mother. My preschool teacher invited me to join her and a few kids on a short trip to the library. My mother stayed behind with the other kids, but when we returned, she was gone. I felt alarmed and abandonded. When my mother picked me up and I told her I was sad that she left, she was annoyed. "How could you think I would stay?" I felt ashamed for not understanding better.

Another day, when I was bit older, my mother and I got into an argument with a lot of shouting. Then she walked out the door and drove away, leaving me alone in the silence. But inside, my mind was filled with loud voices that screamed at me, telling me I was stupid and that it was all my fault that my mother had left. Later the same day after she returned, our neighbor Charlene came to visit, and my mother acted like nothing had happened between us. She even patted my head absent-mindedly, and I felt so relieved. But when Charlene left and I asked my mother what we were having for dinner, she didn't answer. She wouldn't look at me, and it got cold and quiet again. I felt so confused.

Situations like that were very common. My mother always left me alone after a fight with a continued silence the days that followed. It was her way of handling confrontations as well as teaching me when my behavior was unwanted. The silence could go on for days. As I grew older, I got very skilled at reading her and learning to avoid behavior that was unappreciated by her.

The coach analysis

Ninni's mom's silence created a legacy of abandonment

Ninni learned to adapt to this pattern. She internalized the belief that she was the problem, taking all the blame for the fights and arguments that occurred. Over time, the relationship between Ninni and her mother became increasingly distant and emotionally detached.

These experiences made her sensitive to abandonment and silence, causing fear and anxiety whenever she experienced it. **Silent treatment, also known as emotional abuse, can be damaging to children when experienced repeatedly.** The wounds from this type of abuse can last a lifetime, creating an overactive trigger whenever we experience silence from friends, colleagues, strangers, or partners.

The more Ninni experienced those forms of abandonment, the more she internalized the belief that she was to blame. The repetitive nature of Ninni's mother's silence created a constant fear of abandonment in Ninni, leading her to question her own actions and seek even more validation.

The super parent

Children left alone with their emotions without guidance learn that emotions are not welcome and should be hidden. Children whose emotions are dismissed learn to suppress or repress their emotions. Parents who avoid their child's emotions will have children who learn to run away from emotions. A conscious parent offers practical guidance for emotions.

If Ninni's mother had communicated her intentions of leaving her at preschool before the event, Ninni would have still felt sad, but she wouldn't have taken the blame for her mother leaving. After a disagreement, if Ninni's mother had explained why she wanted to be quiet, then communication between them would have been clear, and Ninni wouldn't have taken on the responsibility. If she had said, for example: "I'm too angry right now to talk. But it has nothing to do with you; it's not your fault. I just need a time out. Is it okay if we have personal time for an hour?"

As a parent, by embracing your child's emotions, you can help them learn to understand and cope with their feelings. This is an act of love that can shape the way they communicate and relate to others in a positive way.

Karin is another patient, who like Ninni, came to me with a lot of childhood trauma that had impacted her life. She wasn't aware of the power that her limiting beliefs and damaging memories had on her. She also wasn't aware of the resulting patterns that she was unconsciously repeating, which led to her internal unease and unhappiness. She was open to exploring and healing her pain, as well as sharing her story with others in the hopes of helping them. All names, including hers, have been changed in her stories, but the issues haven't. Through my many years of practice, I have worked with many versions of Ninni and Karin, as their stories are more universal than they at first believed.

Karin's story

The wound and the programming

"I am unimportant, that's why I'm always left out."

I was always filled with a mixture of nervousness and excitement every time I saw my dad, who exuded sophistication and an air of wealth (even though he was actually really poor). My parents divorced when I was five, and both of them moved on to new relationships and started new families. My mom had a baby with her new partner, while my dad and his new wife had twins. I have a vivid memory when I was about ten. I ran down the stairs and out the door, eager to see my dad once again.

But as I approached him, I couldn't help but feel a sense of disappointment as I realized that my dad's passive demeanor was not reflecting the same level of excitement I was feeling. I felt my arms yearn for an embrace, but it never came.

My sister and I went with him to his house, and when we arrived, I quickly ran to my room to avoid greeting his wife, who made me uncomfortable. But when I opened the door to my room, I was shocked to find it empty, and my belongings replaced by the new cribs of my half-siblings. I felt lost and unsure of where to go. I went to my sister's room and sat on her bed, feeling ashamed, silently wondering where I would sleep that night.

Another time, I was outside in the garden at my mom's house. There was a newly planted fruit tree that had three ripe plums. I've always loved plums, and I remember thinking how good they looked, so I picked them and ate them. When my stepfather saw that the plums were gone, he got angry at me and said they were meant for his son, my step-brother. I felt ashamed.

The coach analysis

Karin's father created a wound of invisibility through disengagement

When we are abandoned by a parent, in this case by a father, we risk growing up believing that we are not unconditionally loved and that there is something missing in us to make that possible. We learn the opposite: we can be abandoned at any moment without reason.

With almost half of all marriages ending in divorce today, does that mean that half of all children grow up traumatized by it? Of course not. There are many factors that interact, and what is required to create a trauma is a perfect storm of unfortunate circumstances and behaviors. In Karin's case, there were so many that it came to shape her life and self-image. Her parents' divorce had nothing to do with her, but she feels abandoned by both her parents and replaced. Her father was dependent on the approval and love of his new wife. He wanted to make her happy and prioritized her over his children.

Karin learned that she can be easily abandoned, unloved, and replaced. Her ingrained truth becomes: "I am not important enough." The feeling of not being included or being ostracized becomes traumatic.

The effects of Karin's father's and stepfather's neglect left a deep wound within her. Growing up, she felt invisible, replaceable, and unimportant. Karin constantly searched for validation and attention from others, particularly from men. She was drawn to individuals who showered her with affection and placed her on a pedestal, but these relationships never fully satisfied her innate yearning for love and acceptance. The fact remained that she could only see herself through the lens of her deeply ingrained belief that she was unimportant. This belief became a self-fulfilling prophecy, shaping her experiences and relationships throughout her life. The wound of feeling invisible can run deep and have far-reaching effects, impacting an individual's self-worth and ability to form healthy relationships.

A single traumatic event does not necessarily create deep-rooted beliefs in a person, but over time, these experiences can cumulatively shape beliefs.

The super parent

In the aftermath of a divorce, it can be challenging for a parent to be the best version of themselves. The emotional toll can drain their energy and focus, leaving little room for the extra effort needed to be a "super parent." But it's crucial to understand that being a super parent is about being a pro in communication and handling the tough emotions.

To make the transition easier for kids, it's important to have conversations with them that are light, loving, and easy, rather than deep, serious, and potentially dangerous. Children need to understand that the divorce is not their fault, and that both parents still love them, even if they're not together. Including the child in discussions and making sure they are aware of what's happening can create a sense of security and help them feel like they are a valued part of the new family dynamic. An example of explaining the concept of two households after a divorce in a light and loving way could be: "Sweetie, Mommy and Daddy love you very much. Sometimes, grown-ups have a hard time living together, and that's why we're going to live in two different houses from now on. But don't worry, you'll still have both Mommy and Daddy in your life, and you'll even get to know some new people too! How do you feel about it? It's fine to be scared of the new and uncertain—we all are. Whenever you feel sad or scared, you can come to us and we'll talk and feel it out."

When kids have a confusing or upsetting experience, they don't say, "I had a hard day" or "That really upset me." They either cry, rage, and get upset, or they might already have had experiences that these emotions are not okay, and they have ways of suppressing or coping with the feelings without expressing them. They will also often wait till they feel safe, and then "project" the emotions they are feeling onto a situation (like crying over getting the wrong color cup or when you cut their toast when they want it square!). And so, if we don't realize this, we often miss out on helping them to let go of what is bothering them.

As a parent, it's important to understand the consequence of aligning your feelings and words. When your children sense that what you say and what you feel don't match, they may lose trust in you. It's okay to express sadness or anger, but it's important to do so in a light way without blame. This way, your children learn that it's not dangerous to have emotions, and that they can communicate their own emotions without blaming anyone else or feeling bad for having them. By creating an open, loving environment, your kids will feel comfortable expressing themselves and learning to cope with their emotions in a healthy way.

It's also essential to remember that if you struggle with managing your emotions, your children may pick up on this and start trying to please you to make you feel better. By embracing and processing your emotions in a healthy way, you set a positive example for your kids to follow. Lead by example, communicate openly and honestly, and your children will learn to do the same. Feelings are neither good nor bad; they are energy flowing through us.

Programmed beliefs

What we experienced and felt as children has become the standard within us. Some examples of common unconsciously programmed beliefs are:

"I don't deserve to be loved."

This belief can cause individuals to reject compliments, avoid intimacy, and sabotage relationships. It may lead to a lack of self-worth and difficulty accepting love and affection from others.

"I deserve to be punished."

This belief can result in self-destructive behaviors, seeking out harmful relationships, or feeling guilty for things that are not their fault. It may stem from a sense of shame or a belief in personal shortcomings.

"I am alone."

This belief can cause feelings of loneliness, social anxiety, or a lack of connection with others. It may lead to a belief that no one truly understands or cares for you.

"I am not valuable enough to be loved."

This belief can result in low self-esteem, feelings of worthlessness, and difficulty accepting compliments or gifts. It may stem from a belief in personal inadequacy and a lack of self-worth.

"There's something wrong with me."

This belief can cause feelings of shame, self-doubt, and a constant need for validation from others. It may lead to a belief in personal flaws and a lack of confidence.

"I'm not allowed to be sad."

This belief can result in denying or suppressing emotions, bottling up feelings, or feeling guilty for being sad. It may lead to a fear of expressing emotions and a lack of emotional regulation.

"I'm not allowed to be angry."

This belief can cause repressing anger, feeling guilty for expressing anger, or constantly avoiding confrontation. It may lead to a fear of conflict and a lack of assertiveness.

"I'm not allowed to be happy."

This belief can result in self-sabotaging behaviors, avoiding joy, or feeling guilty for experiencing happiness. It may stem from a belief that happiness is unattainable or undeserved.

"I shouldn't be afraid."

This belief can cause denying fear, avoiding scary situations, or feeling ashamed of being afraid. It may lead to a fear of vulnerability and a lack of resilience.

"I can't take care of myself."

This belief can result in neglecting personal needs, being overly dependent on others, or struggling with self-care. It may stem from a belief in personal inadequacy and a lack of self-sufficiency.

"I am incompetent."

This belief can cause feelings of inadequacy, difficulty starting new projects, or avoiding challenges. It may lead to a fear of failure and a lack of confidence.

"I am excluded."

This belief can lead to feeling left out, isolated, or rejected by others.

"I don't belong."

This belief can lead to feeling like an outsider, difficulty fitting in, or struggling to find a sense of community.

"I have nothing to offer."

This belief can lead to feeling useless, unimportant, or lacking a sense of purpose.

"I am stupid."

This belief can lead to low self-esteem, feeling inadequate, or avoiding new challenges and opportunities.

"I'm not allowed to be stupid."

This belief can lead to perfectionism, constantly comparing oneself to others, or feeling ashamed of making mistakes.

"I have to become something to exist."

This belief can lead to feeling like you need to constantly prove your worth, seeking validation from others, or never feeling like you are enough.

"I am here to make others happy."

This belief can cause individuals to prioritize others' needs and wants over their own. It may lead to neglecting personal needs, desires, and boundaries, and always putting the happiness of others first.

"I become more liked if I don't stand out or speak up."

Individuals who believe this might avoid speaking their minds or expressing their opinions in order to be liked and accepted. This can result in feelings of insecurity and a lack of self-expression.

"I need to perform to be loved."

Individuals with this belief may focus on achieving and performing in order to be accepted and loved. It can lead to feelings of anxiety, pressure, and constant self-criticism, as well as burnout from never feeling like they are doing enough.

"Money causes problems."

People who hold this belief may view money as a source of negativity and associate it with conflict, worry, and stress. This can result in fear around money management and financial insecurity.

"Money is not for us."

This belief can lead to a scarcity mindset and limit financial success and stability. It may result in a belief that you will never have enough money or that financial abundance is only for others.

"You have to work hard for money."

Individuals with this belief might see money as something that can only be earned through long hours, hard work, and sacrifice. It can result in a fear of leisure and pleasure, and a lack of balance in their lives.

"We can't afford it."

This belief may cause people to constantly live in a state of lack, with a focus on what they can't have or do, instead of focusing on abundance and possibilities. It can limit financial growth and opportunities.

Negative parenting behavior: Abandonment

When we have a wound of abandonment, we often go to great lengths to avoid rejection and the pain that comes with it. This can manifest in different ways, such as:

Being overly accommodating: We may find ourselves constantly saying yes to everything, even when it goes against our own needs and desires, just to avoid the possibility of being rejected.

Constantly seeking validation: We may constantly seek out validation from others to ensure that we are still loved and accepted, even when there is no evidence to suggest otherwise.

Being overly defensive: When faced with criticism or feedback, we may become overly defensive as a way to protect ourselves from the possibility of rejection.

Avoiding vulnerability: We may avoid being vulnerable or sharing our true thoughts and feelings with others, as it opens us up to the possibility of rejection.

Staying in toxic relationships: We may stay in relationships that are unhealthy or unfulfilling, just to avoid being alone and rejected.

Trauma bonding: We may unknowingly seek out partners who seems to nourish our unconscious emotional wounds, but actually the imbalance causes deep pain.

These behaviors can be damaging in the long run, as they reinforce our fears of rejection and can lead to further feelings of abandonment and a sense of worthlessness.

2

REPEATING PATTERNS

The cycle of manifesting wounds

Traumatic experiences often lead to the development of unconscious beliefs and defense mechanisms. This can result in a repetition of familiar and potentially harmful situations, as our brain recognizes them as "safe" and familiar, even though they may be sources of continued trauma. This can manifest in relationships, where we may choose partners who exhibit similar traits or behaviors to those of our past traumatic experiences, which results in a vicious cycle of trauma repetition. The key to breaking this cycle is to gain a deeper understanding of our patterns.

Trauma and its impact on our lives can be complex and far-reaching. It can be like a snowball that has been rolling for years, picking up more and more momentum and causing a cascade of programmed patterns and behaviors. This can be difficult to untangle and heal, especially if it has been a long-standing part of our lives. It is important to understand that healing from trauma and breaking these patterns takes time, effort, and dedication. It's like reprogramming and reparenting ourselves, learning to break old habits and form new, healthier ones. This process can be challenging, but it is also incredibly rewarding, leading to a greater sense of self-awareness, self-love, and peace.

Here is a model that illustrates the progression from trauma to beliefs to repeating patterns:

Trauma: The initial traumatic experience or series of experiences that shape our beliefs and behavior patterns.

Beliefs: The beliefs and coping mechanisms that we develop as a result of our trauma. These beliefs can shape our perception of the world and ourselves, and drive our behavior. Examples of beliefs formed as a result of trauma include low self-worth, fear of abandonment, or a need for control.

Repetitive Patterns: Our beliefs drive our behavior, which can result in repetitive patterns that can be harmful or self-sabotaging. These patterns can manifest in various areas of our lives, including our relationships, career, and daily habits. For example, a person with a belief of low self-worth may repeatedly attract partners who are emotionally unavailable, perpetuating a cycle of heartbreak.

PATTERNS

Stuck in a loop?

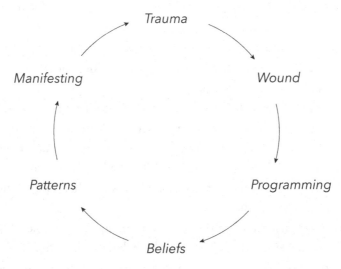

Trauma

Manifesting

Wound

Patterns

Programming

Beliefs

What are you manifesting?

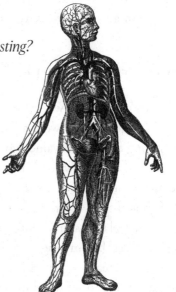

- Wounds stored in the body manifest as passive aggression, apathy, depression, illness, and physical issues.

- Negative beliefs formed in the mind emerge as projections, creating parallel realities.

- Repeated behaviors shape our personality and identity.

- The world reflects this identity, leading to manifestation.

Ninni's story

The unconscious pattern

I remember sitting in the back seat of my mother's car when I was about five. We were on our way to visit my grandmother, and I was going to spend the night. My father had left my mother a year ago. He had fallen in love with Lena and they now lived together. Even though my mother thought she'd be mean to me, Lena was kind. I liked that I was a part of their lives, and that we did things as a trio. We watched movies, ate dinner in front of the TV, and played cards.

It was summer and the warm breeze was blowing in from the open window. I felt happy. Then my mother started talking about my dad. She said she was sad, not for herself, but for me. "You know, I never thought he would leave. I always knew he could, that he had other women, but I thought he loved you too much to ever leave you. That's why it hurt so much when he actually did."

I realized then that my father had left not just my mother, but me. He continued to be unfaithful in all of his relationships after leaving us. And my mother only dated men who were married. I learned early on that men are unfaithful, men leave, and I am someone who will be left behind.

Cycles—repeating patterns

Years passed, and when I was twenty-three years old and madly in love with Michael, I underwent a personality change. In my fixation on him, everything else lost its value. My two best friends became less of a priority for me and they grew frustrated. In the end, they left me and the two of them continued to be best friends. And Michael eventually left me too.

I thought I'd figured it out when I got married. I had close friends and a solid relationship—until I didn't. Nathan's infidelity filled me with anger at first, but my rage was met with silence and coldness. I was not allowed to scream or feel. I had to accept what had happened or else we had no future. So, I buried my emotions so deeply that I could no longer feel them. Instead, I became obsessed with how Nathan was feeling and made sure that he wouldn't leave me. I found countless faults within myself, constantly questioning why he couldn't love me. I took on all the responsibility for our relationship's shortcomings and tried to become someone he could love.

When I met Erik, he was everything I was missing in my relationship with Nathan. He truly saw me. He heard me. He was not afraid of my emotions. And I dared to express them. After Erik's first betrayal, I was allowed to be angry and sad. But I was constantly afraid of being abandoned, as—in my belief—men tend to do. So, I kept a close watch for signs that Erik would leave me and started being strategic about how I expressed my feelings so he wouldn't go. But in the end, he left me anyway. And again, I was reminded that everyone abandons me.

When I fell in love with Erik, he became my entire world. My two best friends, Jenny and Natalie, wondered where I had gone and why I had changed so much. My behavior toward them became very aggressive because I felt left out. In the end, they ended our friendship.

The coach analysis

Protecting yourself through emotional unavailability

When Ninni was a young child, she unwittingly entered into a symbiotic relationship with her mother's pain. Her father leaving her mother was initially neither good nor bad for Ninni, but her mother valued the event as something directly linked to her own self-worth and indirectly linked to Ninni's. The mother's truth becomes Ninni's truth. Ninni learned that she is someone who is left behind and that all men leave or are unfaithful, proven by both parents' relationship patterns.

Ninni's trauma created the programmed truth that "she cannot be loved" and "she is one who is abandoned." Trauma from being abandoned, both by her father, in the case above, and by her mother's silent punishment.

Having a close and honest relationship with one's child is the goal of all parents, but when the line between adult and child becomes unclear and the child takes responsibility for the parent's pain and emotions, it can create wounds, especially if it occurs at a young age. Ninni consciously and unconsciously focuses on not being able to be loved. Her deeply ingrained belief of being abandoned controls her life, so she protects herself by not being honest and vulnerable in her relationships. She also chooses relationships with emotionally unavailable people. This way, she reduces the risk of being vulnerable but increases the risk of being abandoned. By focusing intensely on signs of being left alone, she creates a self-fulfilling prophecy. In the end, being manipulative, not vulnerable, closed up, and passive-aggressive become impossible to love and live with, and she is abandoned.

The super parent

Grief can be scary for a child, but if the grief is pure and honest, it's not harmful. Children get sad all the time, then it passes. It's important to describe feelings without linking them to events. Saying something like "I'm sad because I miss your dad and we're not together anymore" makes the child want their parents to get back together to save their mom from sadness. The parent may also try to protect their child from sadness by pretending everything is okay. But the feeling remains in the room, and when the child picks up on their mom's sadness, they may associate it with themselves instead. Additionally, parents can give their children the space to feel their emotions by acknowledging and validating them, rather than trying to suppress or ignore them. For example, if a child is upset about a situation, a parent can say, "I can see that you're feeling upset, and that's okay. It's normal to feel upset when things don't go as planned." By allowing children to experience and process their emotions in a supportive environment, parents can help them develop healthy coping skills rather than unconscious destructive cycles.

If Ninni's mother had been honest about her pain without blaming Ninni's father (and indirectly Ninni as well), it would have created a sense of security and understanding: "I'm sad, but it has nothing to do with you. Sometimes we're sad; sometimes we're happy. And that's okay."

The emotional availability and consistency of a parent is critical to the well-being and healthy development of children. Children who grow up with emotionally available and consistent parents are more likely to develop into confident and secure adults who have strong self-esteem and are able to form healthy relationships.

On the other hand, children who grow up with emotionally unavailable or inconsistent parents are at risk of developing emotional and behavioral problems that can have a lasting impact on their lives. They may struggle with feelings of abandonment, low self-esteem, and difficulties in forming and maintaining relationships. These issues can follow them into adulthood, affecting their personal and professional lives, and even impacting their own ability to parent effectively.

Therefore, it is imperative for parents to understand the importance of being emotionally available and consistent in their parenting. By doing so, they can help their children develop into well-adjusted adults who are confident, secure, and capable of forming healthy relationships. This, in turn, can have a positive impact on future generations, helping to create a more supportive and loving world for all.

Being an emotionally available and consistent parent can look like the following:

- **Emotional availability:** Listening to and understanding your child's emotions, acknowledging their feelings, and providing comfort and support when they are upset.
- **Consistent attention:** Spending regular and quality time with your child, showing interest in their life, and being present in their daily routines.
- **Clear and consistent boundaries:** Setting clear rules and expectations for your child and maintaining consistency in your parenting.
- **Emotional support:** Encouraging and supporting your child's growth and development, helping them navigate challenges, and celebrating their achievements.
- **Availability for communication:** Encouraging open communication with your child, listening to their concerns, and being responsive to their needs.
- **Consistent follow-through:** Keeping promises to your child, being dependable and reliable, and following through on commitments to your child.

By consistently demonstrating these behaviors, a parent can create a supportive and nurturing environment for their child that promotes healthy development and well-being.

Karin's story

The unconscious pattern

Growing up, I felt like I was constantly caught between two families. I felt like an outsider, never truly a part of either, and always on the fringes. I dreamed of being an only child, with all the love and attention centered solely on me. But instead, I felt like I didn't exist, like a forgotten piece in a jigsaw puzzle. There was my father, his wife, and their two children, who formed one family unit. And there was my mother, her husband, and their two children, who made up another. My sister and I were left to navigate this complicated web of relationships on our own. She was a year older and was coping by taking on the role of the helpful elder sister. And when that didn't work for me, my coping strategy early on was that I needed to fight for attention, always feeling a twinge of shame whenever I did.

I remember when we were kids visiting our cousin's home, and I woke up in my cousin's room. She was two years older and nowhere to be found. She and my sister wanted to sleep together because they were closer in age, and my father wanted me to sleep on the couch. I felt like an outsider, so I screamed until I was allowed to sleep in my cousin's room and my sister agreed to sleep on the couch. When I woke up and found that everyone was gone, I was taken aback. I opened the door and tiptoed out, only to find everyone gathered around the kitchen table, playing games, and laughing. They all looked up as I entered, and my father told me to go back to bed. I obeyed, but I couldn't shake off the feeling of loneliness as I cried in my cousin's room.

Cycles—repeating patterns

At twenty-nine years old, I was a successful chiropractor and one of my clients had grown particularly fond of me. He had been with his wife for seventeen years and together they had a daughter. When he would lavish me with compliments and express his feelings of love toward me, I was flattered, but deep down I knew it was wrong. However, my intense yearning for love and affection overpowered my moral compass and we began an affair. I continued to treat him as a patient, and eventually, when he left his family, I felt chosen, adored, and loved.

On our first date, he took me on a romantic trip to Hawaii, flying first class and showering me with attention and affection. He declared us soulmates, and I felt deeply connected to him. But our fairytale was short-lived. Upon our return, he informed me that his ex-wife needed to move back into their house for a few months, a situation that I found incredibly unsettling. Despite my reservations, he convinced me that it was temporary and that he only wanted to be with me. Unfortunately, our relationship ended after six months with an explosive argument that left us both feeling threatened and deeply hurt.

We reconciled soon after, but his ex-wife made it clear that she did not want me to be around her child. He complied with her wishes, and we broke up once again, this time just a week before Christmas. On Christmas Day, I received gifts worth the value of a car, but instead of feeling grateful, I felt ashamed and unworthy. The pain of being excluded from a family and being someone's second choice was more than I could bear.

The coach analysis

The dilemma of trust and love

Karin has a persistent desire for attention and validation, often unconsciously seeking it in sophisticated ways. This need stems from her fear of rejection and being left out, which has become deeply ingrained in her. Even when her partner shows her love and affection, she is unable to fully see it due to her fixation on feelings of exclusion.

Her lack of trust in love creates a dilemma, as she longs for it but cannot fully recognize it when it is present. Her deeply held beliefs prevent her from fully experiencing and accepting love, perpetuating a cycle of seeking attention and validation without finding the love and acceptance she desires.

Karin often attracts partners who are also struggling with being truthful and honest. At first, she may not recognize this or may choose to ignore it, believing that she can change her partner. However, this belief only triggers her own lack of trust in love, perpetuating the cycle of unfulfilled relationships.

Her partner's struggle with truthfulness only reinforces Karin's belief that she is not worthy of love and acceptance. This, in turn, makes it even harder for her to recognize and accept love when it is present. The combination of her partner's dishonesty and her own insecurities creates a toxic relationship dynamic that is bound to fail.

Despite her best efforts to change her partner and make the relationship work, the cycle of unfulfilled love continues. Until Karin can confront her own lack of self-trust, she will continue to attract partners who struggle with truthfulness. Breaking free from this cycle will require a deep and honest introspection, as well as the willingness to walk away from relationships that are not serving her.

The super parent

To ensure that children feel included and valued, it is important to involve them in decisions that affect their lives and to communicate openly and honestly with them. This helps to build trust and a sense of security for the child. For example, when making changes to a child's room, it is important to involve them in the process and explain the reasons for the change. This could involve asking the child how they feel about sharing their room and making sure their voice is heard in the decision-making process. In this way, the child feels empowered and in control, which is crucial for their overall well-being. It's important to remember that a child will always try to communicate their feelings to you in some way. If they feel like they don't have control over their situation, they may try to make you feel the same way.

By being aware of this and giving the child a sense of choice, such as "Would you like to eat with a spoon or a fork?" or "Would you like to share your room with your younger siblings or your older sister?" you can help the child feel more in control and valued. It's also important to regularly check in with children to see how they're feeling and to address any concerns they may have. This can help to build a strong, trusting relationship between the parent and child and foster a sense of belonging and security.

Children are often very good at expressing their emotions, even if they do not always have the words to articulate them. Children often reflect their own emotions onto others, especially those they are close to, such as parents or caretakers. If a child is feeling left out, for example, they may not communicate their issues or emotions directly, but instead may act distant or withdraw from interactions. If a child feels unloved, they may act out by being mean or uncooperative. It is important for caregivers to be aware of these behaviors and to recognize that the child may be trying to communicate their emotions indirectly.

Nonviolent communication (NVC) is a powerful tool for creating healthy and meaningful relationships, both with others and with oneself. It involves recognizing and expressing one's own feelings and needs, and empathetically listening to the feelings and needs of others. For example, if your child is saying mean things to you, it's important to listen to how they're feeling. They may be feeling upset, angry, or not seen. These feelings can indicate that they need attention and care. At the same time, it's important to listen to your own feelings as well. If you're feeling hurt, this is an indicator that your child may also be feeling hurt, which can help you address the situation in a more compassionate and effective way.

By expressing empathy and understanding, and by being present and open to their feelings, you can create a safe and supportive environment for your child. You can say things like, "I understand that you're feeling hurt right now. I'm sorry for making you feel that way. I love you and you matter to me. I'm here if you need a hug."

By approaching the situation in this way, you can help your child feel heard and validated, and you can work together to find a solution that meets everyone's needs.

Negative parenting behavior: Enmeshed trauma

This refers to a type of emotional trauma that occurs when there is a blurred boundary between a child and their parent, causing the child to take on the responsibilities and emotions of the parent.

This often happens when the parent is unable or unwilling to manage their own emotions and relies on the child for emotional support. Over time, this dynamic can create deep-seated insecurities and self-worth issues for the child, leading to difficulties in forming healthy relationships in adulthood.

Enmeshed trauma can have long-lasting and detrimental effects on a person's mental and emotional well-being.

3

DEFENCE MECHANISMS

Surviving in a dysfunctional family structure

We live in a world where, unfortunately, dysfunctional relationships are a human norm. Some people are aware that they grew up in a dysfunctional environment, but most either don't know or deny that their family system was dysfunctional. We tend to normalize the environment in which we grow up.

When we say dysfunctional, we mean that the way each family member's needs are met is destructive. If a child's fundamental needs are not met because the parents need to fulfill their own interests, such as drinking with friends, the child may develop destructive behavior to get their needs met. The child may try to get the parents' attention by interrupting them, hugging them, or showing them something nice that they have done. If the child's needs go unmet repeatedly, the child learns: 1. My needs cannot be met; 2. I must adapt to the destructive family structure to get them met.

As a result, the child's behavior may become more and more dramatic:

- Acting out becomes their defense and protection from what is dysfunctional by screaming, crying, and demanding attention.
- Isolating becomes their defense and protection from what is dysfunctional by disappearing, running away from home, or isolating from the family.
- Avoiding becomes their defense and protection from what is dysfunctional by adapting and becoming overly helpful.

When parents in a household only see to their own interests and not the child's needs, the family is not a secure enough environment for the child. It's essentially a lack of love and a recipe for pain, conflict, and even abuse. The child then carries this sense of separation into adulthood. They may separate themselves from others. They may sacrifice themselves to meet others' needs or only focus on their own needs in a relationship. As a result, they may live with a partner without feeling satisfied. Clear examples of this are: codependency, love addiction, gambling addiction, sex addiction, work addiction, social media addiction, alcoholism, etc.

Dysfunctional upbringing can take many forms and can have a profound impact on an individual's life.

STUCK IN CHILDHOOD

How do you know?

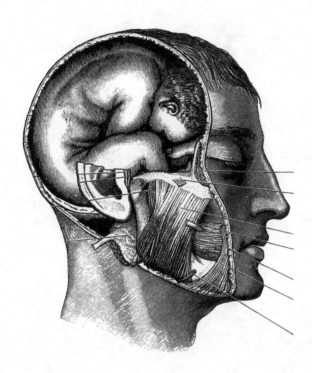

ENMESHMENT:
"I exist to make you (mom and dad) feel loved and happy. I feel guilty if I take anything from you / If I take anything for myself."

DEFENSIVE:
"I need to defend my right to be myself while also belong in the family / group."

AUTONOMY:
"I am my own person, free to express myself and give to myself without feeling guilty."

IN A CHILD'S MIND

My needs can't be met in the family.

↓

Being open and honest doesn't work.

↓

I can't unmet my needs.

↓

I start manipulating to get my needs met.

↓

I mimic what others in the household do —suppressing feelings, creating an alternative reality, being violent, dramatic, or silent—to survive. I either echo their behavior or do the opposite to survive.

↓

New beliefs and patterns form: I feel I need to be destructive, dramatic, intense, or silent to meet my needs.

Ninni's story

Developing a defense mechanism

Growing up, life was always just me and my mother. I believed we were close, but we never really talked about our emotions. We never said "I love you" to each other. It was mainly during fights when we got close to each other. That's when the emotions were strong and we actually did communicate. Our fights almost always ended with me being the one apologizing, which made my mother more loving. As I became a teenager, the fights escalated, and my mother struggled with me being home less and less. "This isn't a hotel," she would often say resentfully.

I was fifteen years old when my mom got a computer, a small Mac with MS-DOS and Word. The internet wasn't around yet, and I mostly used the computer to play games and write essays. One day, when I turned on the computer, there was a document on the desktop that my mom had written. It was titled "Help." I opened it and read my mom's farewell letter to life. She didn't want to go on because her daughter was too difficult and she didn't have a life partner. I responded with an encouraging answer, hoping it would make my mother think twice and take a step out into the world and not focus so much on me. The next time I was on the computer, I received a reply. My mother was angry and frustrated because I didn't give her the answer she wanted most. She wanted me to tell her that I loved and needed her and that I would help more at home. So I wrote my response. During dinner a few hours later, we pretended like nothing had happened. But soon my mother replied on the computer again. This became our way of communicating.

Examples of dysfunctional family structures:

- **Neglect.** Children who grow up in households where their basic needs for attention, love, and affection are not met are often neglected. This can lead to feelings of loneliness, abandonment, and low self-esteem.
- **Emotional abuse.** Parents may use hurtful words, insults, or ridicule to control their children. This type of abuse can cause the

child to feel worthless and may lead to depression, anxiety, and difficulty trusting others.

- **Physical abuse.** Children who experience physical abuse may suffer from physical injuries and emotional scars. This type of abuse can cause fear, shame, and a loss of trust in others.
- **Inconsistent discipline.** Inconsistent discipline can lead to confusion and anxiety for children. They may not understand what is acceptable behavior and what is not, leading to behavioral problems.
- **Blame and criticism.** Children who grow up in households where they are constantly blamed and criticized may develop low self-esteem and a lack of confidence.

These are just a few examples of how a dysfunctional upbringing can look like. It is important to note that the effects of a dysfunctional upbringing can vary greatly from person to person and can continue to impact an individual throughout their life.

A dysfunctional family structure is characterized by a lack of ability on the part of the parents to meet the needs of their children. This is often a result of the parents themselves being victims of a destructive upbringing. The parents may be unconsciously carrying over negative patterns of behavior and relationships from their own childhood experiences.

Becoming aware of a dysfunctional upbringing is a process that can take time and self-reflection. Sometimes we normalize the way we were brought up, and it can be hard to identify that anything was at all problematic. But here are a few examples of what it can result in. Maybe you recognize some.

Signs indicating a problematic childhood experience:

- **Difficulty forming and maintaining healthy relationships.** People who grew up in a dysfunctional family may struggle with intimacy and trust, which can manifest in unhealthy relationships.
- **Love addiction.** Love addiction is a pattern of behaviors and thoughts that revolve around an intense, obsessive preoccupation

with romantic relationships and can manifest as a fear of abandonment or a need for constant reassurance from partners.

- **Low self-esteem.** A lack of validation and support from parents during childhood can lead to feelings of worthlessness and self-doubt.
- **Substance abuse or addictive behavior.** Some individuals may turn to substance abuse or other unhealthy coping mechanisms as a way of numbing or escaping from traumatic experiences.
- **Mental health issues.** Childhood trauma can increase the risk of developing mental health problems such as depression, anxiety, and PTSD.
- **Manipulation.** When you're unable to express your needs because you're afraid of being rejected or disliked, you may resort to manipulation (unconsciously) to have those needs met.
- **Difficulty managing emotions.** Individuals who grew up in a dysfunctional family may struggle with regulating their emotions and may experience intense feelings of anger, sadness, or shame.

The coach analysis

The power of autonomy

Let's say Ninni's mother's identity became solely being Ninni's mother, dedicating her entire existence to the role. As a result, Ninni became the center of her mother's life, potentially causing disruptions to Ninni's mental and emotional well-being. Ninni perceives her mother's sacrifices as selfless, but in reality, her mother may have been driven to prioritize her child due to unfulfilled personal needs for love and validation, lacking it from a romantic partner, friends, or work. This behavior can create an unhealthy attachment bond between the mother and child.

As Ninni grows up, she may develop emotional distance toward people who get too close, or skepticism toward those who express "too much love." This attachment bond and trauma can feel suffocating to Ninni and trigger feelings of discomfort, leading to responses of disengagement or silence. The situation described is an example of an enmeshment attachment.

The super parent

As parents, it's crucial to understand that our children are not ours to control or possess. They are individuals with their own needs, desires, and boundaries. It's our responsibility to support and guide them, but also to respect their autonomy and allow them the space they need to grow and develop. It's important to remember why we chose to become parents in the first place, and that our role is to be a guide, not a boss or owner. **By recognizing and respecting our children's boundaries, we can foster a healthy and supportive relationship and help them grow into confident and independent individuals.**

Examples of respecting a child's autonomy:

- Allowing them to make their own decisions, within reason and based on their age and development.
- Encouraging them to express their opinions and thoughts, even if they differ from your own.
- Supporting their interests and hobbies, rather than forcing them to pursue activities you prefer.
- Giving them privacy, such as allowing them to have their own personal space and time to themselves.
- Avoiding over-controlling or micromanaging their behavior, and instead giving them the freedom to learn and make mistakes.

By respecting a child's autonomy in these ways, you can foster their sense of self, confidence, and independence, and create a relationship built on trust and mutual respect.

Karin's story

Developing a defence mechanism

I grew up with a sister and several half-siblings as a result of my parents' divorce and their second (and third) marriages to others, so I often felt left out. I remember getting ready to compete in a horse jumping competition at the stable one sunny Saturday. I asked my mother if she could drive me there, but she said no. I rode my bike the three miles to the stable and competed with all my heart. I ended up coming in second place and rode home with my prize in my backpack, proud of myself. I was ten years old.

Another day, I called my mother to ask if she could pick me up after playing with a friend. She said no and told me to hitchhike. I walked the five miles back home, feeling tired and frustrated.

The coach analysis

The empowerment of being recognized as a child

Karin took her parents' lack of engagement as evidence that she was not important enough to engage with, leading to feelings of shame for being unimportant. This resulted in Karin creating behaviors aimed at proving her worth. As an adult, Karin works extremely hard for validation, even burning herself out at work. The need to feel special drives her to develop destructive methods to gain love. Despite knowing deep down that she is not important, she still wants to be, which could result in her oscillating between extremes: codependency (excessive reliance on another's approval or affection for their own sense of self) and narcissism (self-focused, stemming from a feeling of worthlessness, usually the byproduct of a dysfunctional childhood).

Individuals with a need for validation may alternate between codependency and narcissism as a coping mechanism for feelings of unworthiness and neglect. A person may act grandiose, seeking attention and validation, then switch to sacrificing their own needs to avoid rejection. This swinging between two extremes stems from the same underlying wound of feeling unimportant and unloved. For example, a person who grew up feeling unnoticed may act boastful and demand admiration, trying to prove their worth to themselves and others. At other times, they may become overly accommodating, putting others' needs before their own in a bid to avoid rejection. These behaviors are driven by fear of being rejected and a belief that their worth is dependent on the approval of others. In this scenario, the person is trying to cope with their deeper emotional wound and insecurity by constantly swinging between codependency and narcissism. When these tendencies become pronounced and interfere with their daily life, it may indicate a personality disorder.

However, it's important to note that codependency and narcissism are not recognized as disorders on their own but rather as patterns of behavior. For example, if an individual has a severe codependency, they may struggle to set boundaries in relationships and become enmeshed with others, losing their sense of self in the process. Or if an individual has a severe form of narcissism, they may lack empathy and exhibit a pattern of exploiting others for their own gain. In both cases, it's essential for the individual to be aware of their part in their relationship failures and to take responsibility for their actions. A complete lack of insight into their own behavior is a hallmark of a personality disorder.

The super parent

A super parent would approach parenthood with a clear understanding of their own motivations and desires. They would ask themselves why they want to become a parent and ensure that their reasons align with providing unconditional love and guidance to their child.

For example, a super parent would not have children simply to fulfill their own desire for a big family, without considering their ability to provide the necessary emotional support and attention to each child. Instead, they would take the time to reflect on their own emotional needs and work toward resolving any unresolved childhood wounds before becoming a parent.

Additionally, a super parent would constantly check in with themselves and their parenting practices to make sure that they are not projecting their own insecurities onto their children. They would strive to be aware of their behavior and how it may impact their children, and actively work toward becoming a more conscious and present parent.

Positive parenting behavior: Listening

Listening to your kids' needs can be a simple yet powerful way to make them feel valued and seen. Here are some ways to do this:

- Make an effort to be present with your children, put away distractions, and actively listen to them when they are speaking to you.
- Let your children know that their feelings are important and matter. Acknowledge their emotions and help them understand and cope with them.
- It's important to let your children make mistakes and learn from them. Avoid overprotecting or micromanaging them, as this can stifle their growth and sense of self-worth.
- Model the behavior you want to see in your children, such as showing empathy and respect and treating others with kindness.
- Show that you care about your children's interests and passions by asking them about them and taking an active role in their pursuit.
- When your kids are talking to you, repeat back to them what they are saying and show that you understand. This can help them feel heard and acknowledged.

4

ATTACHMENT STYLES

How they lead to coping mechanisms

Attachment style is a widely recognized concept in psychology and relationships, and it refers to the ways in which we form and maintain emotional bonds with others. Most of us have a primary attachment style, but it can vary due to the type of relationship we're in. To truly understand your behavior in relationships, it is crucial to identify and understand yours. This knowledge can provide valuable insights into the origins of your attachment behaviors and help you to make positive changes in your relationship patterns. You are not doomed to have one single attachment style your whole life. By exploring our childhood experiences and gaining a deeper understanding of our caregivers' own attachment styles, we can gain insight into our own patterns and make positive changes for the future.

    Examples of the four main attachment styles: secure, anxious-preoccupied, dismissive-avoidant, and fearful-avoidant:

- **Secure attachment style.** People with a secure attachment style feel comfortable being close to others and trust that others will be there for them. They have a positive view of themselves and others, and they feel safe in their relationships. Often, they have experienced consistent, loving care from their primary caregivers during childhood.
- **Anxious-preoccupied attachment style.** People with an anxious-preoccupied attachment style have a strong desire for close

relationships, but they worry about being abandoned or rejected. They may feel insecure in their relationships and may struggle with trust issues. This attachment style can develop in childhood if a child's needs were often inconsistent or if their caregiver was emotionally unavailable.

- **Dismissive-avoidant attachment style.** People with a dismissive-avoidant attachment style value independence and may feel uncomfortable with closeness and intimacy. They may push others away or avoid emotional intimacy, and they may struggle with trust. This attachment style can develop if a child felt their needs were not important or if their caregiver was distant and unresponsive.

- **Fearful-avoidant attachment style.** People with a fearful-avoidant attachment style have conflicting desires for closeness and distance. They may crave intimacy but also fear it, and they may have trouble trusting others. This attachment style can develop if a child experienced inconsistent care or if their caregiver was both available and emotionally volatile.

Ninni's story

Her mother's legacy

Growing up in a small town in Sweden, my mother was part of a family that included her father, mother, an older brother, and a younger sister. Before my mother's younger sister was born, her grandfather contracted polio and became paralyzed in both legs. Despite this setback, he went on to have a successful career and was known for being unfaithful to my grandmother. His presence had a major impact on the family, with all the children looking up to him. He was tough and had a wicked sense of humor, often telling my mother she was pretty but dumb and her sister was ugly but smart. My mother was frequently told that she was a nuisance as a child.

On one occasion, when the family was driving in the car, she was being particularly troublesome and wouldn't sit still. Her father became frustrated and eventually stopped the car, put her out on the road, and drove away. My mother was five years old. When my mother told me this story, she didn't reflect that the experience could have been harmful in any way. In fact, she defended her father by explaining how troublesome she always was, even though she was only five years old at this time.

As an adult, my mother remains a sensitive person. All sounds are too loud, all spaces too cramped, all smells too strong, and other people too much of a disturbance. She reacts to everything. My music, my friends, doors closing too hard, even if I cough before going to bed. Everything worries or bothers her. She rarely communicates these feelings, but communicates them clearly through her body language and facial expressions. She also says other things, like hints and jabs about her disapproval. I learned early on how to read her and predict how I should say, do, and be in order to avoid upsetting her.

The coach analysis

Avoidance of emotions and intimacy runs deep

Ninni grew up with an emotional and highly sensitive mother. But because her mother as a child was taught that she was too rowdy, too loud, too demanding—that her feelings were not allowed—she learned to keep them inside. She learned to avoid her emotions and that it was not safe to share them in a vulnerable way.

Ninni's mother, therefore, developed a dismissive-avoidant attachment style, which means she has a tendency to avoid intimacy and close emotional connections with others. This is due to past experiences or trauma that have caused her to be fearful or anxious about being vulnerable. As a result, she may have learned to suppress her emotions and distance herself from others emotionally in order to feel safer. This avoidance of intimacy can be seen in the way she taught Ninni to keep her feelings inside and not express them. Ninni's mother's attachment style has likely had a profound impact on her own emotional development and relationships, and has also likely shaped Ninni's own approach to intimacy and relationships.

As an adult, Ninni became an empathetic person with anxiety about not being loved. Many can experience her as kind, self-sacrificing, and cooperative. But in reality, this is Ninni's unconscious method of getting love. Therefore, the pendulum swings strongly in both directions: Ninni can have sudden outbursts of rage or take after her mother's behavior with passive aggressiveness and snipes.

Ninni may have developed a dismissive-avoidant attachment style as a result of her relationship with her mother. When her mother was emotionally distant or unresponsive, Ninni may have learned to cope by avoiding intimacy and emotional connection with others.

However, it is also possible that Ninni may have developed both a dismissive-avoidant and an anxious-preoccupied attachment style as a way of coping with her mother's avoidant behavior. In such a case, Ninni may both distance herself from others to avoid potential rejection, and at the same time, anxiously seek out attachment and reassurance from others to compensate for the emotional unavailability of her mother.

In Ninni's adult life, her anxious-avoidant attachment style could manifest in several ways in her relationships:

Difficulty with intimacy: Ninni may struggle with forming close, intimate relationships with others, as she fears being vulnerable and risking rejection.

Avoidance of conflict: Ninni may avoid conflicts and difficult conversations in her relationships, as she doesn't want to face potential rejection or abandonment.

Difficulty with trust: Ninni may struggle with trusting others, as she learned from her childhood experiences that people can be emotionally unavailable.

Independence: Ninni may value her independence and autonomy in her relationships, as she has learned to rely on herself for emotional support.

At the same time, Ninni's anxious attachment style could also impact her relationships in the following ways:

Need for reassurance: Ninni may constantly seek reassurance and validation from her partner, as she may fear being rejected or abandoned.

Jealousy: Ninni may experience feelings of jealousy and insecurity in her relationships, as she fears losing her partner to someone else.

Difficulty with boundaries: Ninni may struggle with setting healthy boundaries in her relationships, as she may fear pushing her partner away.

COPING MECHANISMS

Behaviors That Turn into Personalities

Self-sacrificer

Overachiever

Confirmation seeker

Perfectionist

Boundless

Victim

Manipulative

It's complex, isn't it? That's why talk therapy often takes years to fully comprehend ourselves. However, somatic (embodied) work may take less time, and the spiritual route may be the quickest path to understanding.

In today's world, we often talk about "bypassing" when our body, mind, and spirit aren't in alignment. That's why it's important to engage in cognitive work with our minds (understanding our behaviors and recognizing our triggers), somatic work with our bodies (releasing emotions), and spiritual work (recognizing our connection with others, nature, and events).

Somatic (embodied) work can involve a range of techniques and practices, including bodywork, movement, breath work, mindfulness, and meditation. It is based on the idea that the body holds onto and processes emotional experiences, and that addressing these experiences through physical sensations can help individuals release emotional and psychological blocks.

Spiritual bypassing is a term used to describe a tendency to use spiritual practices and beliefs to avoid dealing with difficult emotions, unresolved psychological issues, or challenging life circumstances. It is a form of avoidance that can manifest in different ways, such as denial of one's own feeling, judgments or criticisms of others who are struggling, or an obsession with positive thinking.

The super parent

The importance of creating an authentic sense of self refers to the importance of discovering and being true to one's own values, beliefs, thoughts, and emotions, rather than trying to be someone one is not. Having an authentic sense of self is crucial for leading a fulfilling and meaningful life, as it allows individuals to establish a strong sense of self-worth, self-acceptance, and self-confidence. It can also help individuals form healthier relationships, as they are able to communicate their needs and boundaries effectively.

However, creating an authentic sense of self can be a challenging process, especially for those who have learned to suppress their true selves in order to fit in or be loved. It often involves facing one's own fears, insecurities, and vulnerabilities, and learning to accept and embrace them.

Getting to know what one wants and needs can be a journey of self-discovery, and there are several steps that can help in this process.

Examples of how to feel in your needs:

- **Practice self-reflection.** Ask yourself questions like, "What do I enjoy doing?"; "What makes me feel fulfilled?"; "What do I value most in life?" This self-reflection can help you gain a deeper understanding of your desires and needs.
- **Cultivate mindfulness.** Mindfulness is a practice that involves paying attention to the present moment and being aware of one's thoughts, feelings, and bodily sensations. This can help you become more in tune with your inner experiences and gain a clearer understanding of what you want and need.
- **Practice self-compassion.** Treat yourself with kindness and compassion. Rather than criticizing or shaming yourself, try to focus on self-acceptance and self-love.
- **Seek support.** This can be incredibly helpful in gaining a deeper understanding of your desires and needs.

Karin's story

Her mother's legacy

Growing up in various foster homes, my mother had a challenging childhood. Abandoned by her drug-addicted parents at just five years old, she and her two sisters were placed in an infant home. They were eventually split up and sent to different cities, leaving my mother feeling scared, abandoned, alone, and unloved. Even after being taken in by Ingrid and Josef, it seemed that they were more interested in financial compensation than in truly raising a child.

Yearning for love and stability, my mother got married at the young age of fifteen and had her first child the following year. Her childhood experiences had left her confused and without a sense of belonging. Her mission in life became building the family she never had.

The coach analysis

Not trusting love runs deep

As an adult, Karin's mother has been married four times and consistently put her husband's needs ahead of her own and her children's. Her deep longing for love often takes over, and she may not always be actively interested in her kids' lives and activities. Despite this, she consciously wants her kids to see all the things she does for them and can sometimes feel like a victim of parenthood.

Karin's mother never experienced a secure attachment in her childhood, due to her lack of connection with her biological and foster parents. As a parent, she struggled to form a bond with her own children. To receive love, she may have demanded attention or complained, and ultimately developed an addiction to love, sacrificing everything for her husband's affection.

This addictive pattern was passed down to Karin, who also became addicted to love, making it the center of her life and taking priority over everything else. Unfortunately, both Karin and her mother have a history of not receiving love and have a hard time trusting it, leading to difficulty in forming and maintaining secure relationships. They may end relationships easily when they don't feel loved, perpetuating their cycle of addiction to love and difficulty with trust.

When something has been passed down from generation to generation, it's known as intergenerational transmission. This can refer to the transmission of a wide range of experiences, including bad habits, trauma, cultural values, beliefs, and behaviors. Intergenerational transmission can have a significant impact on individuals and families, as it can shape how they perceive the world and interact with others.

The super parent

Raising children is one of the hardest jobs in the world and changing an attachment style is a lifelong process. It can take generations for a family to heal and change their attachment style, and not everyone has the resources or time to seek therapy.

Karin's mother could have taken these steps to create a bond with her children:

- Awareness.
- Self-reflection.
- Build a secure attachment.

Breaking the cycle of attachment style can be a difficult but rewarding process.

Examples of breaking the cycle of attachment:

- **Awareness.** The first step is to become aware of your attachment style and how it has influenced your relationships. Understanding your attachment style will help you recognize patterns in your behavior and provide a starting point for change.
- **Self-reflection.** It is important to reflect on past relationships and experiences to understand how your attachment style has affected your ability to form close and lasting connections. Ask yourself questions like, "Why do I feel the way I do in relationships?" and "What has been my pattern in past relationships?" This self-reflection can be a powerful tool in understanding the root of your attachment style and can provide valuable insight into how you can change it.
- **Build a secure attachment.** The final step is to actively work on it. Those with an avoidant attachment style often end up with an anxious partner and vice versa. It's important to recognize who you are drawn to and why. If your attachment style has caused you a lot of pain, it's essential to consciously seek out individuals with a secure attachment style to foster a healthy relationship.

Making changes to one's attachment style doesn't have to happen overnight. Taking small steps, such as setting boundaries, learning to communicate effectively, and practicing self-care, can lead to significant changes over time. However, it is important to remember that no one is a victim in this process. Each person has the power to change and make a positive impact in their life and relationships. Karin is not a victim of her mother's attachment style, she has the power to seek help and make changes in her own life. Similarly, Karin's mother can look at herself with empathy and compassion, understanding that she, too, has the ability to change and heal. It is never too late.

Unhealthy coping mechanisms

Unhealthy coping mechanisms are those that provide temporary relief from stress or difficult emotions, and are created to basically cope with emotions. They can have negative long-term consequences.

Examples of unhealthy coping mechanisms:

- Substance abuse, including alcohol and drug use.
- Overeating or undereating.
- Withdrawing from social connections and support.
- Engaging in risky or dangerous behaviors.
- Self-harm, such as cutting or burning.
- Passive-aggressive or anger outbursts.
- Excessive spending or gambling.
- Compulsive behaviors, such as checking or cleaning repeatedly.

These are some common daily dramatic coping mechanisms that people may engage in unconsciously to meet their needs.

There are also coping mechanisms that may be less noticeable and less extreme.

Examples of unconscious daily coping mechanisms:

Need: To feel enough
Coping strategy: Overachiever

Overperforming is a strategy to feel enough. Good grades, good salary, good title, many "followers." In romantic relationships, this person is very hard on themselves. When it comes to their own healing, they are frustrated that it's not happening fast enough. They have a lot of shame, and see their uncomfortable feelings as a weakness they cannot get rid of.

Need: To feel worthy
Coping strategy: Perfectionist

A person who does everything themselves. They demand perfection in themselves and others. They are constantly developing themselves, fixing and delving into all methods and techniques to get the relationships they want. Unconsciously, they act in their relationship the same way they do at work. They are up in their heads and are often disconnected from their body. Their judgment of others who do not meet their standards is a reflection of their lack of self-acceptance.

Need: To feel safe
Coping strategy: Boundless

They make the relationship the most important thing in their life. Their life, identity, and priorities revolve around the relationship. Their partner becomes the only one who can make them feel good. If the relationship is unstable, they feel unstable too.

Need: To be heard
Coping strategy: Victim

They have been traumatized and have not healed. Even if they are aware of their past relationship, their subconscious still associates love with pain. They do not believe they can trust anyone and feel it is not safe for them to open their hearts. They stop dating, or date busy people who will not fall for them. In this way, they avoid being vulnerable and risking being hurt.

Need: To be validated
Coping strategy: Confirmation-seeking

They use confirmation as medicine. They feel alive with high doses of dopamine and love and unconsciously create drama to reach strong emotions, regardless of what those are. They avoid real intimacy and vulnerability and exist and act in various extremes such as codependency and narcissism.

Need: To be authentic
Coping strategy: Manipulative

They give to get. All actions have a hidden agenda, perhaps even unconsciously. They are strategic in their actions and expect the same in return. They are suspicious of others' actions and believe that there is always a hidden motive.

Need: To be seen
Coping strategy: Self-sacrifice

They do everything for their relationship but still feel abandoned and unappreciated. They want and need more investment from their partner. They focus on others' needs more than their own because they do not feel worthy of having their own needs met. They believe that sacrificing themselves will eventually lead to love and acceptance.

When we rely on unhealthy strategies to meet our needs, we risk damaging our relationships and our own well-being. This can lead to feelings of anger, frustration, or resentment toward others, and can create a vicious cycle of behavior that is difficult to break.

When we communicate our needs clearly and assertively, we are more likely to get our needs met and to experience deeper, more meaningful connections with others.

Positive parenting behavior: Providing fundamental needs

By fulfilling a child's fundamental needs, you can create a secure attachment style. As a parent, one of the most important tasks is to provide for the basic needs of your child. When these needs are met in a healthy and consistent manner, it lays the foundation for a secure attachment style. These basic needs are:

- **Safety.** This includes providing a safe and secure home, with a roof over their head and enough food to eat. Children need to feel safe and secure in their physical environment.

- **Acceptance of emotions.** Children need to know that their feelings, whether positive or negative, are accepted and validated by their parents. They should feel free to express their emotions without fear of judgment or rejection.

- **Validation of emotions.** Children need to feel seen and understood. This involves listening to their thoughts and feelings, and being present for them in both good times and bad.

- **Guiding emotions.** Children also need help in understanding and managing their emotions. This may involve teaching coping skills and helping them to identify and regulate their emotions.

- **Physical touch.** Physical touch, such as hugs, cuddles, and holding hands, provides a sense of comfort and security for children.

When these needs are met in a healthy and consistent manner, children develop a secure attachment style that allows them to trust and rely on their parents. This foundation of love and security is crucial for positive emotional and social development, and sets the stage for healthy relationships later in life.

5

SURVIVAL STRATEGIES

Ways for escaping suffering

Many of us are disconnected from our emotions. This means that we don't know what we're feeling, how we're feeling, or why we're feeling it. It also means that we struggle to be present with our emotions in our bodies. We desperately try to escape all uncomfortable emotions. Why? Because we were never taught that they are safe or how to manage them.

Imagine a tiger catching a zebra. You've seen the zebra running for its life and fighting to survive. But in the moments when the tiger has its claws in the zebra, the zebra looks calm, even though it is still alive. The zebra has left its body. It has dissociated from its own body to escape the pain of dying. Now, imagine that we humans also do this, but our biggest threat is not a tiger but the feeling of being abandoned, rejected, wrong, neglected, disappointed, etc.

We disconnect and dissociate and start focusing on something outside of ourselves to feel satisfaction and handle the stress.

- We look for confirmation by posting on Twitter, Instagram, Facebook, etc.
- We look for entertainment and satisfaction from Netflix, alcohol, and games.
- We look for instant gratification by shopping, overeating, and scrolling the internet.

Unlike the zebra's calm, when we leave our bodies, we may feel restless or unfocused. Our primal instincts, such as fight, flight, freeze, and fawn are activated when we're in our so-called trauma response. These responses are believed to be evolutionarily ingrained and have helped humans to survive in dangerous situations in the past. Some people, such as those with PTSD, live in a state of constant trauma response.

Fight response occurs when an individual perceives a threat and feels that they can physically defend themselves. This might manifest as an increase in adrenaline and the sudden urge to physically fight the source of the perceived threat. For example, if someone was being physically attacked, their fight response might kick in, and they would physically defend themselves.

Flight response occurs when an individual perceives a threat and feels that they need to escape to safety. This might manifest as a sudden increase in adrenaline and the urge to run away from the source of the perceived threat. For example, if someone was in a situation where they felt they were in immediate danger, their flight response might kick in, and they would try to escape to a place of safety.

Freeze response occurs when an individual perceives a threat and feels that they cannot physically defend themselves or escape. This might manifest as the person becoming physically paralyzed, either temporarily or permanently. For example, if someone was in a situation where they felt threatened and saw no means of escape, their freeze response might kick in, and they would become physically frozen or paralyzed.

Fawn response occurs when an individual perceives a threat and feels that the only way to stay safe is to appease or submit to the source of the perceived threat. This might manifest as an individual becoming overly compliant or submissive to the source of the perceived threat. For example, if someone was in a situation where they felt threatened by someone in a position of power, their fawn response might kick in, and they would become overly submissive to try to avoid further harm.

Dissociation refers to the process of becoming disconnected from one's thoughts, feelings, sensations, and surroundings. Dissociation is a common response to emotional distress and can take on many forms. A person who has been rejected by a romantic partner may feel intense emotions of sadness, hurt, and anger, but in order to survive these feelings, they may dissociate from their body. They may start to feel numb and emotionally detached, and they may struggle to remember details of the rejection. Over time, if this pattern of dissociation continues, it can become a chronic experience such as depression.

A person who has experienced neglect as a child may dissociate during arguments or confrontations as a way to survive the overwhelming emotions they are feeling. They may feel like they are outside of their own body, watching the situation unfold, instead of fully experiencing it. This can be a protective mechanism, allowing them to avoid the emotional pain and anxiety associated with the situation.

In both cases, dissociation is a survival strategy for dealing with emotional distress. This can make it difficult to form meaningful connections with others, and to experience life in a meaningful way.

When we are present, we are better able to process our thoughts and feelings and make sense of our experiences. When we are fully engaged and focused, we are better able to listen, to understand, and to empathize with others. Moreover, being present helps us to be more mindful and to appreciate the simple pleasures in life. It allows us to savor the moment and to experience the world in a more vivid and meaningful way, which is crucial for our mental and emotional well-being.

Dissociation can have a major impact on our ability to be present and fully engage with our experiences. Uncovering and managing our unconscious survival strategies is a journey worth taking. By exploring these patterns, we can gain a greater understanding of ourselves and develop a greater presence in our lives. Let's delve into this.

SURVIVING

What do you do when your existence and connection feel threatened?

Flight ⟶ *Fight* ⟶ *Freeze* ⟶ *Flaw*

Ninni's story

The survival strategy

I don't remember when it happened, when I gave up on my dad, but I shut down early. I never needed him, his help, or his love. I knew better than to ask for it. That realization came so early that I don't remember any way of relating to him. When people are open and ready to love me, I pull away. I become disgusted. I've therefore only attracted people who maintain a certain distance, who don't show too much love or tenderness. It feels safe. Ideally, I am alone. Then no one can hurt me and I don't have to relate to another person's feelings for me.

The coach analysis

Inauthenticity with emotions as a survival strategy

The betrayal of Ninni's father leaving her mother for a younger woman and the feeling of abandonment likely triggered her survival strategy: to feel only mild disdain and irritation toward her father (which later turned into disdain for men who try to give love to Ninni).

It is possible that Ninni's father was not able to feel his emotions and therefore became inauthentic, which created a separation between them that made it impossible for Ninni to connect with her father. Her father may have had so much pain and guilt from the divorce that he distanced himself from his feelings. Ninni unconsciously picked up that distance and responded to it with even more distance. She also became inauthentic with her emotions. The void grew.

This can also make it feel unsafe for Ninni to express love with compliments, touch, and tenderness—all forms of closeness. It may feel so unfamiliar and unknown that she becomes uncomfortable. She may, therefore, sabotage these opportunities by closing herself off, by being cold, or even more clearly: be only attracted to men with whom she doesn't have to feel vulnerable. Men who are unavailable in one way or another, either because they are not in touch with their emotions or because they are involved in another relationship.

Ninni's father's dissociation from his own emotions has likely contributed to Ninni's own emotional dissociation. She was convinced that she didn't need him and that he didn't mean anything to her as a survival strategy to avoid feeling sad or abandoned. In doing so, Ninni has distanced herself from her own emotions, creating a barrier between herself and the pain she feels. She becomes inauthentic to her own feelings.

Inauthenticity with emotions as a survival strategy means that a person may suppress or hide their true emotions to protect themselves in a particular situation. For example, in a relationship, someone may put on a facade of happiness, even if they are feeling sad or frustrated, to avoid conflict or to keep their partner from leaving. This can become a pattern, where the person is consistently inauthentic with their emotions, and they may not even be aware that they are doing it.

In childhood, a person who has dissociated from their emotions in response to feeling rejected or hurt may exhibit behaviors such as withdrawing from others, avoiding intimacy, or acting out in disruptive ways. They may have difficulty forming close relationships and may struggle with feelings of loneliness and insecurity. As they grow older, this pattern can continue and manifest in different ways. They may struggle with trust and intimacy in romantic relationships.

These behaviors and emotions are often a result of past experiences that have led to a survival strategy of dissociating from emotions and being inauthentic with emotions.

Examples when being inauthentic has become pathological:

- **Suppressing or denying their emotions.** An individual may try to hide or downplay their emotions, even if they are feeling intense sadness, anger, or fear. They might believe that showing these emotions is a sign of weakness and opt to put on a brave face instead.
- **Using humor to deflect from their emotions.** A person might use humor to distract from their emotions and keep conversations lighthearted. This could be a way for them to avoid dealing with difficult emotions that are too overwhelming to process.

- **Being passive-aggressive.** When someone is passive-aggressive, they may express their emotions indirectly through actions or hints rather than directly communicating them. This could be a way for them to avoid confrontation or facing their emotions head-on.
- **Pretending to be happy.** An individual may pretend to be happy when they are actually feeling sad, lonely, or angry. This could be a way for them to protect themselves from others seeing them in a vulnerable state.
- **Projecting their emotions onto others.** A person may project their emotions onto others by accusing or blaming them for their feelings, rather than taking responsibility for their own emotions. This could be a way for them to avoid facing their emotions and deal with the source of their discomfort.

The super parent

Vulnerability refers to the quality of being exposed to the possibility of harm or damage, often in a psychological or emotional sense. When it comes to relationships, being vulnerable means opening up and sharing our deepest thoughts, feelings, and fears with others, even if it makes us feel uncomfortable or exposed. This level of openness is crucial for developing deep connections and intimacy, as it allows us to truly understand and connect with the people we care about.

However, being vulnerable can be incredibly difficult. It requires us to confront our own insecurities, to let go of our defenses, and to trust others with our most vulnerable parts. Despite these challenges, vulnerability is critical to building healthy, meaningful relationships. Without vulnerability, relationships become shallow and lack a sense of true connection.

Examples of how to be vulnerable with your kids:

- **Share your own thoughts and feelings.** Let them see when you cry. Let your kids see that you're not afraid to be vulnerable and that you're willing to open up and share your own experiences with them.

- **Be honest about your mistakes.** It's important to model honesty and accountability for your kids. If you make a mistake, own up to it and talk to your children about what you learned from the experience.
- **Encourage open communication.** Let your kids know that they can come to you with anything, no matter how big or small, and that you're there to listen and support them.
- **Practice self-reflection.** Take the time to reflect on your own experiences, feelings, and thoughts. This will help you better understand your own emotional state and be more in touch with your own vulnerability, which will make it easier to be vulnerable with your kids.

Honesty vs. vulnerability

It is also important to know that being honest and being vulnerable are two different things. Honesty refers to telling the truth about a situation or how you feel, while vulnerability refers to exposing your deepest fears, emotions, and insecurities to others. Being honest in a relationship is important as it builds trust, but it does not necessarily mean that you are also being vulnerable.

Someone can be honest about the fact that they are unhappy in the relationship, but they may not be willing to be vulnerable by admitting why they are unhappy or what their deepest fears are. This lack of vulnerability can create a barrier in the relationship and prevent the development of a deep intimacy. In such cases, it can also lead to a projection, where instead of facing and expressing their own fears, the person projects their own negative feelings onto their partner. For example, instead of admitting their own insecurity, they may accuse their partner of not being attentive enough.

Therefore, it is important to be both honest and vulnerable in a relationship in order to build a deep connection and achieve true intimacy. When both partners are open and willing to share their feelings and insecurities, they can build a stronger bond and understanding of each other. This helps to create a sense of safety and trust in the relationship.

A behavior or thought pattern becomes pathological when it interferes with daily functioning and causes significant distress in one's personal and professional life. For example, in a relationship, if jealously becomes so excessive and intense that it leads to obsessive checking, constant interrogation, and controlling behavior, it can be considered a pathological form of jealously. This can strain the relationship and cause harm to both partners.

Karin's story

The survival strategy

I moved out on my own when I was fifteen years old. I had my own apartment, which cost $100 a month. I received housing support from the government and also worked at a café. I was on my own, without my parents. I was free, happy, and thriving. But I also felt unsupported and lonely.

I asked my mother if she could help me pick up some furniture I bought at a flea market. She didn't have a car and told me to ask my friends. However, my friends were also fifteen years old. I felt too embarrassed to ask their parents for help, and I felt ashamed that my parents wouldn't help me. I felt unloved and a burden. At that point, I stopped asking for help, or if I did, it was more in an indirect way. It was too painful to be rejected, so I learned to be my own best supporter.

The coach analysis

Control and masculinity as a survival strategy

Growing up without support from her parents, Karin became independent at an early age. She had to fend for herself and grow up without the guidance of her parents. This led her to becoming self-sufficient at a young age. She also took on traits of toxic masculinity as a result of growing up without a caring father figure. She became controlling, selfish, hard, cold, and insensitive. To find a healthy balance of masculinity, which includes leadership, protection, support, rationality, stability, and safety, she needed to seek help. And that is not so common for a fifteen-year-old.

Karin also struggled with her feminine side. Being soft, open, warm, and empathetic has been a challenge for her. Instead, she experienced the shadow side of femininity, which includes being triggered, overwhelmed, angry, and scared. This is a result of not having a nurturing mother figure.

To protect herself from vulnerability, Karin took control in most situations and dictated the terms, which led her into relationships where the man may not have had a sense of secure authority, like her father, or a lack compassion and tenderness, like her mother. Karin's inner conflict of wanting help and support, but also feeling the need to do everything on her own, led to overprotecting herself. This manifested in controlling behavior in relationships, refusing to ask for help, or unconsciously pushing people away to avoid the possibility of getting hurt.

An example of this might look like: In a relationship, Karin may dictate the terms of the relationship and become controlling and demanding. She may also avoid expressing her emotions and struggles, as she doesn't want to appear weak or vulnerable. This can lead to a lack of intimacy and depth in the relationship, as she struggles to let her guard down and be vulnerable.

The super parent

As a parent, you hold a profound responsibility for your child's life to provide a secure and loving place for them for the first eighteen years of their life. Divorce and inconsistent parenting often instills deeply ingrained survival strategies within children.

Karin's dad was absent from her life to the extent that he was no longer involved; one might even say he suffered from an avoidant disorder. Her mother, focused on her own survival strategies, left Karin to become her own parent. This led Karin to develop numerous survival strategies, resulting in a toxic self-reliant demeanor. What her parents could have done, but failed to do, was to provide the necessary support and nurturing as she grew up, fulfilling the roles of both a caring mother and supportive father figure.

As a result, Karin had to assume the role of parenting herself, initially from a wounded place. She felt ashamed to seek help and believed she was undeserving of support and love. However, this ultimately led her to experience burnout as she struggled to ask for help. At this crossroad, she realized the importance of engaging in healthy self-reparenting. She rebuilt herself with a focus on self-worth, self-love, and becoming a nurturing and supportive figure.

This involved relying on her own support while also allowing others to assist her. Karin learned to nurture herself and incorporate self-soothing techniques into her journey. She also opened herself up to receiving help from others, trusting that their support was based on her inherent worthiness. This self-exploration and healing journey was a long one for Karin, taking her a span of ten years to fully engage in self-reparenting.

Her story serves as a reminder of the crucial role parents play in their children's lives. As a father, it is important to provide support, structure, and material safety for the children. As a mother, nurturing them emotionally is essential. In cases of divorce or the absence of one parent, this delicate balance is disrupted, often causing profound challenges for both parents and children. When a parent is absent, it can inflict deep emotional damage upon the child, resulting in trauma responses to be ingrained at an early age.

If someone is unconsciously repeating trauma responses (fight, flight, freeze, and fawn) in their daily life, it can manifest in several ways.

Examples of trauma responses:

- **Chronic anxiety.** If someone's trauma response is to always flee or escape danger, they may experience chronic anxiety in their daily life, even in situations that are not inherently dangerous. This could manifest as feelings of nervousness, panic, or an urge to escape or avoid certain situations.
- **Aggression.** If someone's trauma response is to always fight perceived threats, they may exhibit aggressive or hostile behavior in their daily life, even in situations where this behavior is not warranted. This could manifest as anger, impulsiveness, or the tendency to lash out when feeling threatened or challenged.
- **Dissociation.** If someone's trauma response is to freeze in the face of danger, they may experience dissociation in their daily life, where they feel detached from their surroundings or their own thoughts and feelings. This could manifest as feelings of emotional numbness, a sense of disconnection from the world, or difficulty focusing and staying present in the moment.

- **Codependency.** If someone's trauma response is to always submit or appease perceived threats, they may engage in people-pleasing behavior in their daily life, even in situations where this behavior is not necessary. This could manifest as a fear of confrontation, a tendency to avoid expressing their own needs and desires, or a pattern of sacrificing their own needs for the sake of others.

Humans have developed various survival strategies over the course of evolution to protect and dissociate themselves from uncomfortable emotions. These strategies can range from simple habits like excusing, blaming, and shaming to more complex strategies like denial and projection.

Examples how we use survival strategies and dissociation from emotions:

- **Repression.** Pushing away discomfort and anxiety from consciousness. Emotions avoided: Anxiety, discomfort.
  Example: Sarah's parents had a tumultuous relationship, and she has repressed the memories, leading to trust and attachment issues in her adult relationships.

- **Intellectualization.** Viewing things in a rational, detached way. Emotions avoided: Empathy, connection with emotions.
  Example: Chantelle is able to logically understand why her partner is upset with her, but she has difficulty feeling empathetic and connecting with the emotional aspect of the situation.

- **Self-Deception.** Turning a negative thought into its opposite. Emotions avoided: Anger.
  Example: Clara loves her children but unconsciously hides anger toward them. This self-deception can manifest in subtle ways such as passive aggression or irritability.

- **Excusing.** Blaming failures on external circumstances. Emotions avoided: Responsibility, guilt.
  Example: Isla finds it difficult to communicate with her partner and blames it on their busy schedules, rather than taking responsibility for the lack of effort in making time for each other.

- **Ostrich Behavior.** Ignoring facts to blind oneself. Emotions avoided: Acknowledging problems, guilt.
  Example: John and Jane are in a relationship, and John refuses to acknowledge that he has a drinking problem. Despite multiple arguments and discussions with Jane, he continues to ignore the situation and deny that there's a problem.

- **Projection.** Blaming others for one's own actions. Emotions avoided: Accepting responsibility, guilt.
  Example: David constantly argues with his partner and blames them for his own insecurities and unhappiness. Instead of taking responsibility for his emotions and actions, he projects his faults onto his partner.

- **Self-Blame.** Taking on negative properties or feelings perceived as one's own. Emotions avoided: Blaming others, guilt.
  Example: Mikael blames himself for his parents' divorce and feels guilty.

- **Beautification.** Using language or behavior to downplay or hide unpleasant thoughts, emotions, or actions. Emotions avoided: Confronting unpleasant realities, guilt.
  Example: Maria portrays her destructive divorce as simply growing apart, and Derek portrays his firing as an exit.

- **Undermine/Overvalue.** Attributing overly negative or positive traits to oneself or others. Emotions avoided: Accepting one's own abilities and faults, self-esteem issues.
  Example: John constantly undermines his own abilities and sees himself as a failure, regardless of his achievements. He may also overvalue the abilities of others and sees them as superior to himself.

- **Romantic Fantasies.** When life becomes a constant hope for change that never comes, individuals may cling onto romantic fantasies. Emotions avoided: Disappointment, frustration.

Example: Karl believes that if his wife shares his interest in nature and outdoor activities, their relationship will improve and they will live the life of his dreams. Katarina believes that once she loses 7 kg., she will meet her soulmate. Sofia believes that if her husband goes to therapy and addresses his aggressive behavior, their relationship will improve.

- **Self-harm.** People avoid emotions by punishing themselves with external means. Emotions avoided: Painful emotions.
  Example: Dawn experiences deep self-loathing and starves herself to avoid feeling the self-loathing. Sofia feels disconnected and anxious and seeks refuge in destructive sexual relationships.

- **Melodramatic.** The strategy here is to draw attention to oneself and express emotions in a theatrical way. Emotions avoided: feeling powerless, neglected, or invisible.
  Example: Kajsa expresses her feelings but no one listens. She stamps her feet and dramatically leaves the room by slamming the door.

- **Disconnected.** Avoids acknowledging mental problems by separating the event and feelings from each other. The strategy here is to keep the emotions at bay by not allowing them to surface.
  Example: Elizabeth makes the feelings from a sexual assault inaccessible, while the cognitive aspects remain. She can describe the assault in detail with apparent calmness, but finds it difficult to have sex.

- **Humor.** Avoids difficult emotions by using humor to brush them off. The strategy here is to find temporary relief from anxiety and fear through laughter.
  Example: Kris is feeling overwhelmed by work and the responsibilities of daily life. Instead of facing these emotions head-on, they says things like, " I think I'm officially turning into a caffeine-dependent robot." By using humor, they hope to relieve some of the tension they are feeling and avoid having to confront the root of their anxiety.

- **Black and white.** Avoids feeling uncertain and insecure by creating a "on or off" behavior. The strategy here is to create stability and avoid a mediocre situation by constantly shifting between two extremes.

  Example: Tina has been in a relationship for a year. One day she is madly in love and wants to get married, while the next day she wants to end the relationship. Christian dates and finds love every third month. Every new woman is "the one," but he often ends the relationship after a few months.

While these survival strategies can provide temporary relief, they often prevent us from fully addressing and healing the underlying wounds.

It's all the parent's fault, right?

We have given you a few examples of events from childhood that have shaped our behavior in adulthood. This does not mean that everything is the fault of our parents, that we are victims, and they are the scapegoats. But everyone has experiences from childhood that have shaped us in one way or another. We must dare to look at our childhood and upbringing with critical eyes, to become aware of what set the ball in motion. We must dare to question our parents and their actions to ultimately realize that they are just as human as we are and to forgive and accept what has happened. No parent can be an ideal parent all the time—and certainly not a super parent. The examples we give of how the super parent would have acted are meant to contrast what happened to us with an ideal version of what could have happened. But also, to bring comfort to ourselves and the little child inside us that may still be hurting.

Our parents are people with their own experiences, traumas, and programmed truths about themselves. Based on their history, they do the best they can—just like we all do. We just want to illustrate how behavior can be shaped, based on what happens when we are young children. It is an explanation, nothing more. What has happened has happened, and it's nothing we can change today. Rather, we can try to create an understanding of our parents' own feelings and experiences and how they have shaped them just as much as they have shaped us.

What we can do, however, is be honest with ourselves about how we handle life today. Shine a light on how our programmed truths about ourselves limit us in life. We can break the cycle. At least for the traumas that we, our parents, and our ancestors have created. Of course, we will create new ones, just as our children after us will. But that is life, and we owe it to ourselves and those who come after us to do our part to become the best version of ourselves.

Positive reparenting behavior: Shadow and somatic work

Shadow work and insight work are powerful tools for personal growth and self-discovery. By engaging in shadow work, you become aware of the parts of yourself that you have repressed or denied and gain a deeper understanding of your unconscious motivations and behaviors. This can be a transformative process, as it allows you to shed light on the parts of yourself that have been hidden in the shadows.

Insight work is about taking the knowledge gained from shadow work and turning it inward. It's about exploring your thoughts, feelings, beliefs, and patterns of behavior to gain a deeper understanding of who you are and what drives you.

Shadow work and insight work are important steps, but they are just the beginning. YES, we know, it IS a lot of work, and not everyone chooses to evolve because of not knowing where to start or how to start.

By learning to allow your emotions, you can take your journey of self-awareness to the next level. **Somatic (body) work offers a unique approach to self-exploration and healing.** Rather than relying solely on the mind and cognitive understanding, it invites individuals to listen to their bodies and explore what is stored within. This type of work recognizes that our bodies hold onto memories and experiences.

If you're someone who doesn't enjoy learning through your mind, that's okay! Did you know that you can learn through your body instead? That's where somatic work and meditation come in. By taking the time to listen to your body, you can gain valuable insights into what needs healing. It's like your body has its own language, and it will communicate with you—sometimes loudly—through chronic diseases, aches, and pains. **You don't really have to understand complex definitions like trauma response, survival strategies, and shadow work. Your body will tell you what needs attention and care. All you need to do is listen.**

Meditation is a powerful way to foster a stronger relationship with yourself rather than just enhancing the practice itself. **This book offers different meditation forms (in Part 3) to help you get to know yourself better.** Over time, you can develop your own meditation practices, guiding yourself, and eventually, others as well. There is no one-size-fits-all approach; try it out, tailor it to your needs, trust yourself, explore, and forge your own path with it. You are strengthening your intuition, not the coach's.

PART 3
THE PRACTISE

1

YOUR EQ MUSCLES

Talk therapy, also known as psychotherapy or counseling, is about the cognitive understanding of one's thoughts, patterns, triggers, feelings, and behaviors. Emotional work, on the other hand, is a process of self-healing that involves developing a deeper understanding of your emotions and how they impact your life. Talk therapy leads to awareness and insight but doesn't always lead to change. Cognitive behavioral therapy (CBT) can be a quick fix and help us modify our destructive behaviors, but it doesn't always address the root cause and heal us.

In order to achieve sustainable growth and change, it's necessary to add the next step of the process: Emotional Work. This healing journey involves releasing suppressed emotions and cultivating feelings of compassion, understanding, acceptance, and love toward our bodies. These are often the emotions that were missing during our traumatic experiences. **By allowing ourselves to fully FEEL and acknowledge our most vulnerable part, we can begin to heal and move forward in a new way. This process can be difficult and not linear, but it is essential for transformation.**

The body and mind are closely interconnected and influence each other in countless ways. Emotions, thoughts, and physical sensations are all interwoven and affect each other in real-time. For example, when we are stressed, our bodies respond with physical symptoms such as increased heart rate, sweating, and muscle tension. Similarly, physical experiences can shape our emotions and thoughts. For instance, if we have a positive physical experience such as a massage, it can result in a sense of relaxation and well-being. This, in turn, can positively impact our thoughts and emotions, making us feel calm and happy.

Falling in love also has a profound impact on our body and mind. Research shows that when we fall in love, our brain releases high levels of serotonin, dopamine, and oxytocin, which create a feeling of euphoria and pleasure. You might have noticed that this surge of feel-good chemicals also leads to physical changes, such as a glowing skin, brighter eyes, and a more attractive appearance. On the other side, heartbreak can lead to high levels of stress and anxiety, which can cause physical changes, such as dark circles under the eyes, a tired complexion, and even premature aging.

The body and mind are constantly communicating with each other, and what happens in one system affects the other. This interplay between the body and mind is why emotional work can be so effective in promoting healing.

Here are some of the most popular ways to do embodied emotional work:

Body-oriented psychotherapy: This type of meditation combines traditional talk therapy with physical techniques, such as healing and touch.

Somatic experiencing: This kind of meditation focuses on helping individuals gradually process and integrate their traumatic experiences by bringing awareness to the sensations in their bodies.

Bioenergetic analysis and mind-body bridging (MBB): This kind of meditation uses breathing techniques to help individuals become more aware of the relationship between their emotions and mind. It is based on the principle that the body and mind are interconnected, and the physical sensations in the body can provide clues to our unconscious material.

When we suppress our emotions, they will, with time, start to manifest as physical symptoms such as headaches, back pain, and even chronic conditions like gluten intolerance. Through emotional work, we can learn to understand the emotional roots behind these physical symptoms and release the suppressed emotions. This is done through various techniques. For example, in emotional release work, we might explore the feeling and allow ourselves to fully experience it, such as feeling anger and expressing it through screaming. By doing this, we bring awareness to the emotional suppression and start the process of releasing it to reduce or even eliminate the physical symptoms associated with it.

Mind-body connection

The connection between emotions and physical symptoms is a complex and fascinating topic. It's widely recognized that when we experience stress or negative emotions, our bodies release stress hormones like cortisol, which can impact our physical health and lead to symptoms such as increased heart rate, elevated blood pressure, and muscle tension. When we suppress emotions, avoid feeling our feelings, push them, away and ignore them, they might transform into chronic health issues such as digestive issues, migraine, allergies, etc. To better understand the connection between emotions and physical symptoms, it's important to be in tune with our bodies and to pay attention to how our emotions are impacting our health. By doing this, we can begin to understand the root cause of our symptoms.

There are some common physical symptoms that may be experienced during periods of emotional stress, which can include:

- Shallow breathing or shortness of breath
- Increased heart rate and blood pressure
- Muscle tension or stiffness
- Headaches or migraines
- Nausea or digestive issues
- Fatigue or insomnia
- Sweating or chills
- Skin rashes or hives

When we experience emotional stress over an extended period, it can start to result in the emergence of chronic physical issues that may persist even with intervention.

Here are some physical symptoms and what the common emotional reason behind it may look like:

- Headaches: tension, stress, anger, stuck in a limited mindset.
- Back pain: feeling unsupported, carrying too much responsibility for too long.
- Neck pain: holding onto anger, feeling constricted. Mind is disconnected from the emotional body.

- Shoulder pain: feeling burdened, carrying emotional weight.
- Hip pain: fear of moving forward, insecurity, fear of change.
- Knee pain: fear of moving in any direction, controlled, not flexible, fear of change.
- Foot pain: fear of moving forward or take leadership/ownership, fear of change.
- Stomach pain: fear, anxiety, worry, hard to digest ideas or directions.
- Intestinal issues: feeling stuck, holding onto emotions.
- Chest pain: holding onto emotions, feeling constricted.
- Arm pain: feeling weighed down, feeling burdened.
- Hand pain: feeling like you have to "do it all" or have a hard time letting go.
- Throat pain: hard time expressing values and needs.
- Mouth pain: difficulty speaking up or expressing emotions.
- Teeth pain: biting off more than you can handle, grinding, suppressed anger.
- Ear pain: difficulty hearing or receiving messages, feeling unheard.
- Sinus pain: feeling blocked, holding onto anger.
- Skin issues: feeling vulnerable, exposed, fear of being seen.
- Joint pain: feeling stiff, holding onto rigid beliefs or attitudes.
- Temple pain: feeling overwhelmed, holding onto tension.
- Thigh pain: fear of change or moving forward.
- Calf pain: fear of change or moving forward.
- Ankle pain: fear of change or moving forward.
- Elbow pain: feeling burdened or weighed down.
- Wrist pain: feeling burdened or weighed down.
- Fingers pain: feeling burdened or weighed down, powerless.
- Nose pain: feeling blocked, holding onto anger.
- Jaw pain: holding onto tension, grinding—can be linked to sex organs.
- Cheek pain: feeling vulnerable, exposed.
- Heart palpitations: feeling overwhelmed, anxiety.
- Shortness of breath: feeling overwhelmed, anxiety.
- Nausea: feeling overwhelmed, anxiety.
- Dizziness: feeling overwhelmed, anxiety.
- Fatigue: feeling overwhelmed, burnout.

- Insomnia: feeling overwhelmed, anxiety.
- Migraines: holding onto anger, stress, lack of self-power.
- Irritable bowel syndrome (IBS): feeling stuck, holding onto emotions, difficulty processing emotions.
- Fibromyalgia: holding onto tension, feeling burdened.

By listening to our own bodies, we can tap into a wealth of information and guidance. In fact, our bodies often hold the answers to questions that our minds may struggle to understand or address. By working directly with our bodies, we can create a powerful and transformative healing journey.

Different states of mind

To begin the healing process, we invite you to first understand the different states of your mind. Scientific research has shown that our conscious mind represents only about 5 percent of our total mind, while the remaining 95 percent lies within our unconsciousness. The conscious mind is responsible for processing our immediate surroundings and generating conscious thoughts, but it has limited access to the vast amount of information stored in our subconscious mind. This information includes our long-term memories, beliefs, attitudes, and emotions, which can have a significant impact on our thoughts, feelings, and behaviors, even if we are not consciously aware of them.

Brain waves

Our brain operates at different frequencies known as brain waves, which are associated with different states of consciousness. These are the main types of brain waves:

- **Alpha** brain wave frequency is typically associated with a relaxed, meditative state of mind.
- **Beta** brain wave frequency is where the conscious (thinking, alert) mind operates and is faster and more active.

- **Delta** brain waves are slower brain waves (like theta) that are typically associated with deep sleep and meditation. These brain waves are also linked to accessing the subconscious mind.
- **Gamma** The gamma brain wave frequency is associated with heightened states of consciousness, such as those experienced during intense focus or moments of deep insight.
- **Theta** brain waves are slower brain waves (like delta) that are typically associated with deep sleep and meditation. These brain waves are also linked to accessing the subconscious mind.

The subconscious mind is a part of our mind that operates below the level of our conscious awareness. It includes information that we are not currently thinking about, such as long-term memories, beliefs, attitudes, and emotions. While the conscious mind operates at the beta brain wave frequency, which is faster, the slower delta and theta brain waves can allow us to access the unconscious mind and bring up repressed emotions and memories.

Through practices like meditation or hypnotherapy, you can learn to access these slower brain wave states and tap into the subconscious mind. This can help you gain insight into your underlying thoughts and emotions. By accessing the theta mind, you can develop a deeper understanding of yourself.

In addition to the slower delta and theta brain waves associated with the subconscious mind, there are also higher frequency brain waves, alpha and gamma, that are associated with different states of consciousness.

Your lower self and higher self

The lower self represents our innermost desires, fears, and beliefs, and is associated with the subconscious mind. By accessing the lower self through alpha or theta brain waves, you can explore their inner world and gain insight into your emotions, beliefs, and patterns of behavior.

The higher self represents our connection to something greater than ourselves and is associated with the superconscious mind. By accessing the higher self through gamma brain waves, you can tap into their inner wisdom and spirituality, gaining a greater sense of purpose and direction in your life.

Access your subconscious

To access your subconscious theta brain wave, find a quiet, comfortable place where you can sit or lie down. Close your eyes and relax your body. Take a few deep breaths to calm your mind.

Focus on your breathing. Pay attention to the sensation of the air moving in and out of your body. Use this as an anchor for your mind and keep your focus on your breath.

Start to slow down your breathing. Make your breaths deeper and slower. This will help to activate the parasympathetic nervous system, which is responsible for relaxation and rest.

Begin to mentally repeat a mantra, word, or sound. This can be a conscious loaded word like "love," "peace," or a neutral unknown word like "mallo," "sessoss," "tallin," or a more spiritual connected word (Sanskrit) sound like "om." Repeat it slowly and calmly in your mind.

Keep your focus on your breathing and mantra. Let your mind wander as you continue to repeat the mantra. As your mind calms, you may start to feel a sense of peacefulness and relaxation. Try to use the same word every time to create a body memory around this word.

Maintain this meditative state of mind. From here, your self-discovery starts. Ask yourself a question, listen, and see what comes up.

By doing this meditation, you can train your brain to slow down its activity, move into a state of deeper relaxation, and reach the subconsciousness.

The real shift

Insight—healing—integration

The first part of this book explores the unconscious aspects of Ninni's life. The second part focuses on gaining insight and understanding, while the current section is centered around the healing process. We call this the final stage, but it is actually a lifelong journey and one that we embark on alone. It may become easier with time and new positive habits may develop, but the process of integrating new understandings and behaviors is an ongoing and ever-evolving endeavor.

The three phases:

Therapy/insight: This phase involves gaining a deeper understanding and recognition of one's personal history and becoming aware of patterns in behavior. It involves gaining knowledge and an understanding of the reasons behind why we behave in certain ways.

Emotional work/healing: This phase involves allowing oneself to experience emotions that have been suppressed. This can include sadness not expressed, compliments not acknowledged, or any other emotions that have been pushed aside. This process of healing involves acknowledging and processing these repressed emotions, which can be both positive and negative in nature.

Change/integration: The final phase involves integrating new and positive behaviors into your life, and replacing destructive patterns with healthy ones. This transformation requires a shift in mindset and a commitment to long-term growth and development. It's not an easy or quick process, but it leads to a more fulfilling and positive life. We refer to this process as "light work," not because it's easy, but because it feels like the opposite of shadow work. Light work can be even more challenging than shadow work for some people. It involves cultivating and embracing new energies, which can be difficult to maintain and requires a deep level of commitment and self-discipline.

Somatic work involves accessing this information through the body, and it can be done through different practices, such as meditation, body-centered therapy, and emotional release. The goal is to create space for the body to communicate with us and help us understand the root cause of physical symptoms and how they are related to our emotions.

It is crucial to remember that accessing this information is not always easy, and it may take time and patience to uncover the deep-seated traumas and emotions that are stored in our body. In the next chapter, we encourage you to exercise your EQ muscles through meditations.

2

EXERCISING YOUR EQ MUSCLES

The relationship between emotions and physical symptoms can differ significantly from person to person, and the unique connection between the two can be explored through deep emotional work such as meditation.

Backdrop meditation is a powerful practice that allows you to delve into your past, embracing whatever arises, and reparenting yourself with the compassion that may have been missing. In this chapter, you will explore a variety of meditation techniques that support the exercise of your EQ muscles.

These methods do not need to be followed in a specific order; feel free to experiment with different approaches and see what resonates with you. Whether you choose to dedicate daily sessions for years or use them as needed depends entirely on where you are in your personal journey.

The essence of meditation often transcends specific goals; it serves as a practice of being fully present.

Backdrop meditation, while aligned with this purpose, offers a slightly different focus by inviting you to explore and release suppressed emotions—a transformative cleanse for your mind and body.

By engaging in this process, expressing and releasing what has been held within, you create space to embrace light, harmony, ecstasy, gratitude, love, and joy—emotions that often lay dormant within us. It's essential to remember that after engaging in shadow work, we must not linger but progress towards cultivating gratitude and love, not only for ourselves but also for all that surrounds us, including figures from our past.

Practicing backdrop meditation requires time and dedication. Allocate a quiet, undisturbed environment where you can fully immerse yourself. You may choose to lie down with a flat spine or sit up—whatever promotes a sense of alignment and comfort. Be mindful of the importance of maintaining a flat spine, avoiding the use of a pillow. Aim for an uninterrupted hour, although the duration can vary based on your experience.

After the meditation, consider journaling as a way to deepen your self-awareness and facilitate the integration of your experience. These written reflections can be immensely valuable in your ongoing journey of growth and transformation. They provide an opportunity to explore your inner world, gain insights, and nurture a profound connection with yourself.

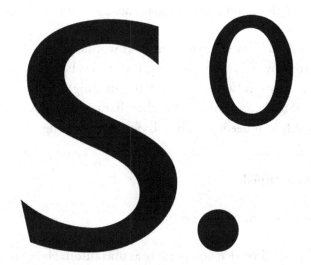

Self-Care

Backdrop meditation: How to transform your wounds.

Step 1: Insight. Finding the original trauma.

When we are dissociated from our emotions because they were too difficult to feel or because we cannot put a name to them, they become mostly a feeling of discomfort. With this process, you can trace the anxiety to understand what feeling you are experiencing and why. We will use our theta mind to enter the subconscious to find stored memories that have had a huge impact on us and create triggers and destructive behaviors today.

Step 2: Healing. How to transform your wounds.

Once you have found the memory, the process begins by healing it by feeling the feelings and adding an adult (reparenting) healthy self-soothing perspective into the memory. Remember that your process is unique and unfolds exactly as it needs to. There is no right or wrong way to do it.

Meditation outlined

Focus on the uncomfortable feeling.

Think of a feeling that you perceive as uncomfortable in your life right now, such as jealousy, feeling excluded, a conflict, or something similar. Something that is active now. Focus on the discomfort and where in your body it feels most intense. Allow yourself to be in this feeling without any defense (protection) such as distraction. Say silently to yourself: "It's okay for me to have this feeling right now. It's safe for me to stay in this feeling." This can feel unbearable, and your job is to stay in the feeling. Allow yourself to fully feel and stay in the feeling.

Travel back in time

Next step, say to yourself: "Take me back to the time when I first felt this feeling." Continue to repeat this to yourself: "Take me back to when I first felt this feeling." For a novice meditator, it may take some time to trust the intuitive signals, as they are always there but can be hard to see. That's why it's so important to be in theta state when doing this exercise. Your subconscious will now retrieve the origin of the feeling, when it was born. There are two ways to reach the memory. One with intuition or with the conscious. The consciousness is limited and may not find the memory, or it may retrieve a memory that is already well-known to you. The intuition can retrieve an unknown memory, often seemingly trivial, that you may not see as having a direct connection to the feeling. This is really good. You will make the connection later. Give yourself time.

Working with the memory

Once you have found your memory, do not hesitate to decide that this is the memory you will work with, regardless of whether it comes from intuition or consciousness. There may be much doubt, criticism, and insecurity of what is what. This is normal. Now, see if you can explore the memory and get into details. This can also feel uncomfortable, which is why it's important to feel it, and that also indicates that you are in a wound. See if you can play a longer version of the memory. Look at the younger version of yourself from the outside. What does the little version of you feel: sad, happy, surprised, frustrated, scared? Do any of these feelings remind you of what is activated in your life right now?

Reparenting

As an adult, try to enter into this memory to change the child's perspective. Fill in the missing gaps for the younger version of yourself. Continuously nurture this part of you by reparenting your younger self. Give the child what they need, talk to them, allow them to express their emotions through feeling, crying, or screaming. Provide a safe space for them. Remember that you are now grown up and in control. The goal is not to relive the trauma, but rather to release the suppressed emotions and bring comfort. This is where the healing takes place.

Repeat this process whenever an uncomfortable feeling arises.

Example:

Sandra has anxiety about a business presentation. She often feels nervous around public speaking and wants to understand why she is triggered. When she goes through the process of finding her memory, she returns to when she was eight years old and had to read aloud in class. She read incorrectly and everyone started laughing. When Sandra goes back to the memory as an adult, she sits next to the younger version of herself in the school desk and as everyone starts laughing, she rubs Sandra's back and says, "It doesn't matter that they're laughing. They're not laughing at you, they're laughing with you. Everyone can make a mistake and it doesn't matter. They don't think less of you for it." Then, the adult Sandra asks the younger Sandra to read again, and when she reads correctly, everyone applauds her for accomplishing the task. Sandra has now changed her perspective from fear to safety in the memory. What remains with Sandra is that she's afraid of embarrassing herself. When Sandra sits with that fear she starts to resolve it. Little by little.

Self-Awareness

Backdrop meditation: How to transform your unconscious self.

Step 1: Insight. Discover your biggest shadow.

Breaking up can bring to the surface our deepest fears and childhood wounds. It is a vulnerable and exposed time when we experience detachment, abandonment, and rejection on multiple levels. As we navigate through this difficult period, it's common for the wounds and fears that we've carried since childhood to resurface. These fears are often the things that we consciously or unconsciously try to avoid, and they can become our biggest hidden fear.

Step 2: Healing. How to transform your unconscious self.

In this exercise, we will identify your biggest overlaying shadow.

Meditations outlined

Close your eyes and enter a meditative state. Think about a romantic relationship you have had, and focus on the moment when it ended. How did it feel?

Repeat the exercise until you have considered at least four different relationships and the emotions you experienced at their end. Identify common denominators among the emotions you experienced during the breakups. These could be feelings such as panic, bitterness, guilt, shame, control, jealousy, doubt, worthlessness, despair, anger, etc.

Reflect on your childhood memories. Try to see if this feeling was present in your life then as well. If so, it is likely that this overall shadow has been present for a long time.

Your most uncomfortable feeling

Practice embracing your most uncomfortable feeling. The feeling that was common to all of your breakups. This is your shadow feeling, your most familiar unwanted feeling. We're going to delve into the subconscious to find the memory that still evokes the same feeling in us today.

Practice being in the feeling

Now, we're going to practice being in that feeling. Close your eyes and embody it as best you can. Remember when you've felt it, feel how it feels. This can be difficult because you've probably dissociated from the feeling because it's also your most uncomfortable feeling. See if you can locate where in the body it sits. Take your time. When you have, see if you can focus on that body part. This may cause you to feel pure physical pain in the area you're focusing on or to feel pain somewhere else. Follow the pain and focus on its path. Stay in the pain and feel it. Now it might become unbearable because the pain in the body is linked to the feeling. Stay in it. See if you can put your hand on the place where it hurts and stroke yourself so you feel warmth and love, or try pressing the place with both hands and breathing out, deeply. Try to vocalize the feeling. Finish by trying to give the feeling a little love, for example, by accepting it, understanding it, feeling it, or just feeling warmth toward the area where it feels. If you can't find where in the body the feeling sits, try taking a deep breath and the body part where the breath stops is often where the feeling is located. Then just continue breathing and focusing on that body part. If you're in alpha and theta, it's likely that memories related to the feeling will now come up.

Examples:

Patrick (age 45) has had five relationships, and every time a relationship ended, he felt hopeless and helpless. When he reflects on his childhood, he realizes that these feelings dominated his life. These are his shadows. The opposite of his shadow, his light and healing, is likely hopefulness, empowerment, and encouragement, which he probably finds challenging to experience and express.

Chantelle (age 35) feels lonely every time a relationship ends. If she reflects on her childhood, she realizes that she felt alone and on her own. Loneliness is her shadow, and it is where she feels most familiar. Chantelle's happiness lies in the opposite of loneliness, which is solidarity. However, this feeling is unfamiliar and therefore scary, shadow work for her involves learning to be in a state of solidarity.

Lars (age 50) feels doubt and indecision every time a relationship ends. This is his shadow, and doubt is his most common feeling. When he reflects on his life, he realizes that this feeling of doubt has been present in many aspects of his life, such as shopping, where he avoids making decisions by buying multiple items, or in his job, where he has wanted to quit for a long time but has been unsure. Shadow work for Lars involves facing and overcoming his doubt to make decisions by making decisions.

Sarah (age 30). Whenever Sarah ends a relationship, she feels a strong sense of anger and frustration. When she looks back at her childhood, she realizes that she felt frustrated and angry at her parents for not paying enough attention to her. Anger and frustration are her shadow. Sarah's light and healing lie in the opposite of her shadow—peace and calmness. However, Sarah feels insecure in this unfamiliar state and needs to work on embracing peace and calmness in her life.

David (age 40). Whenever David ends a relationship, he feels a sense of guilt and shame. He feels that he has done something wrong and is to blame for the relationship ending. When he looks back at his childhood, he realizes that he felt guilty and ashamed for not being good enough or living up to his parents' expectations. Guilt and shame are David's shadow and most visited and felt emotions. To heal and find happiness, David needs to embrace the opposite of his shadow—self-acceptance and self-love. This is an unfamiliar state for him, and he will need to work on embracing this feeling in his life.

Lucy (age 25). Whenever Lucy ends a relationship, she feels a sense of despair. When she looks back at her childhood, she realizes that she felt out of control and deeply sad when her parents went through a difficult long-lasting divorce. Despair and out of control is Lucy's biggest shadow. To cope with this, she started to control everything. To release her shadow, Lucy needs to embrace the opposite of her shadow—trust, surrender, and positivity.

These are just a few examples of what one's shadow feeling may look like and how it can impact their life. It's important to remember that everyone's shadow feeling/state is unique to them and that the process of healing and embracing the opposite of one's shadow feeling or state can be a long and challenging journey.

S.²

Self-Perspective

Backdrop meditation: How to transform your coping mechanism.

Step 1: insight. Discover your programming.

Here are some of the most common unconscious programming that may have arisen from your trauma.

Circle the ones that you instinctively feel are true for you. Circle the ones that you unconsciously act upon.

- I don't deserve to be loved.
- I deserve to be punished.
- I am alone.
- I am not valuable enough to be loved.
- There is something wrong with me.
- I am not allowed to be sad.
- I am not allowed to be angry.
- I am not allowed to be happy.
- I should not be afraid.
- I can't take care of myself.
- I am incompetent.
- I am an outcast.
- I do not belong.
- I have nothing to offer.
- I am stupid.
- I am not allowed to be stupid.
- I have to become something to exist.
- It is my responsibility what others feel; I have to take responsibility for others' feelings.
- I am here to make others happy.
- I will be more liked if I don't see and hear myself.
- I need to perform to be loved.
- Money causes problems.
- Money is not for us.
- You have to work hard for money.
- We can't afford it.
- You have to save your money.

Step 2: Healing. How to transform your coping mechanism.

Choose one of the programmed truths that you circled. Close your eyes and enter into an alpha state. Say your truth, such as "money is not for me" and feel the sensation of saying it to yourself. Stay with that feeling and fully embody it, even if it feels unbearable.

Ask yourself when this became true for you. For example, when you were six years old and you wanted a toy and your mother said that you couldn't afford it, or when you were seven years old and wanted something and your father said you could only have it if you were good. Both of these situations could have led you to the start of the belief that you are not worthy of money.

When the memory arises, try to enter the memory and change your perspective on it. For example, even though your father said, "You can only have it if you're good," that is not true. You don't only get money when you're good. See if you can tell the child version of yourself that they are worthy of money, with an adult perspective. Ask the younger version of yourself what they want right now. It could be an ATM card with all the money in the world that they can use as they please. Stay with your younger self as they experience the opposite feeling and give yourself a new truth, such as "I have an abundance of money."
It's important to be patient with yourself during this process and remember that it may take time to fully internalize a new perspective.

Meditation outlined

Choose a limiting belief or negative thought.
Enter into a relaxed state, such as alpha, by closing your eyes.
Say the belief out loud and pay attention to how it feels.
Allow the feeling to fully sink into your body.
Identify when and how the belief became true for you.
Imagine yourself stepping into the memory and changing your perspective.
Give yourself a new, empowering belief.
Hold onto the new perspective and imagine feeling empowered and loved.

Full circle

The optional next step in the process is to visualize a gathering of all the people who were involved in creating the programming. This includes your younger and older self, as well as others who have triggered these feelings over the years. This practice can be very revealing and powerful.

Have everyone involved sit in a circle.

Ask each person to take responsibility for the programming/belief they have projected onto you. Connect with their higher selves.

Allow the younger self to express their needs and make sure they are fulfilled by your higher self before leaving the visualization.

The older self can then return and open their eyes.

Example:

Greg grew up feeling insecure and constantly questioning himself. As a child, he was often made fun of, which caused him to doubt his worth and wonder if there was something inherently wrong with him. This feeling only grew stronger as he got older, and he became increasingly self-conscious about everything he said and did, always seeking validation from others. Even now, as an adult, he still feels nervous and anxious in social situations, worried that others will laugh at him if he says the wrong thing or does something embarrassing. This fear has become deeply ingrained in him over the years, and it's hard for him to shake it off.

To help overcome this limiting belief, Greg can try the daily practice of changing his perspective. He can start by entering the wound: saying out loud, "I'm someone you make fun of" and sit with that and see what comes up. Then, he can enter the memory of being made fun of and imagine telling the younger version of himself that he is worthy of love and acceptance, despite what others may have said or done.

By holding onto this new perspective and giving himself a new truth, such as "I am fun and that is safe," Greg can start to reprogram his beliefs and overcome his self-doubt and anxiety in social situations. It may take time and practice, but with patience and persistence, he can break free from the limitations of his past experiences.

With practice, it will become a second nature for you to see when you are in your programming (trigger) and shift your perspective and adopt new, more empowering beliefs. It will require less effort and become more automatic as you continue to work on changing your mindset.

S.³

Self-Acceptance

Backdrop meditation: How to transform contempt.

Step 1: Insight. Discover your repressed aspects.

Write down an aspect in a person in your life that you find annoying. Instead of saying "Kim is very judgmental," write your name. Answer the question: Why do you resist this aspect? This often leads to an internalized truth. Examine if this truth is still true for you.

Step 2: Healing. How to transform contempt.

Imagine the person who annoys you as a reflection of yourself. If you can't find the aspect within yourself, it may be deeply suppressed and blind to you. You have separated yourself from an aspect of yourself and you have become blind to your own manifestation.

Meditation outlined

Close your eyes and focus on an aspect of yourself that you dislike.

Allow yourself to feel the discomfort and contempt associated with this aspect.

Recall the first time you came in contact with this aspect or trait within yourself.

Keep in mind that answers are received in alpha, theta, or gamma states, not in beta state, which is used for asking questions. Relax and allow the answer to come to you in the form of a memory, inner knowing, or feeling.

If you find yourself searching frantically for the memory, you are still in beta and may be having trouble feeling the emotion. Take some time to meditate and reach a meditative state of mind.

Once the memory surfaces, observe it and try to understand why you resist seeing that trait in yourself.

Examples:

Linda is bothered by her colleague because she is fake. She laughs falsely, never says what she thinks. She says "yes" but radiates "no," and talks behind her friends' backs. Linda is bothered by her colleague because her own view of herself is honest. When she asks herself why she has resistance to seeing herself as fake and authentic, the answer quickly comes to her: "One must not be fake."

Going back in time to when this belief was formed, Linda finds herself in a memory of her stepfather giving her a disapproving look when she reached out for more food at the dinner table. He didn't say anything, but Linda felt like she had done something wrong and didn't know what. And this was not the first or last time she felt this from her stepfather. This created insecurity in Linda about not knowing what others think. To this day, she is triggered by mixed signals. She has unconsciously created a ban on falseness. It is a threat to her and she copes by guessing rather than asking. She defends herself by avoiding confrontation (the same as her stepdad did). Most likely, all people are both clear (direct) and unclear (indirect)/ honest and fake, including Linda. However, because Linda has created a ban on the trait, she can't see it in herself. This becomes her suppressed characteristic.

By allowing herself to think, "I am fake/indirect," she can connect with the emotion it creates. It's important to fully allow the feeling. Linda must allow herself to feel indirect and avoidant. By accepting this reality, she will also be able to accept others with the same characteristics. She will start seeing her colleague with compassion, but she will most likely only be able to do this after she has been able to do that with herself.

In essence, you can have a value of being authentic and still allow yourself and others to be imperfect. Witnessing is more powerful than judging. **Self-acceptance is more powerful than self-criticism.** By judging others harshly, you are also judging yourself harshly. It might be worth taking a closer look at this. Another crucial aspect to consider is that we may unconsciously attract people who remind us of someone who has treated us poorly in the past. While it can be challenging, it's important to recognize when these dynamics are at play and evaluate whether we want to continue in those relationships. At times, these relationships can serve as a learning opportunity, but it's okay to walk away when they no longer serve our growth and well-being. It's essential to approach this decision with compassion for ourselves and for the other person involved.

Ron struggles with feeling inadequate. He can never seem to measure up to his own expectations, let alone those of others. This makes him judge others and get triggered when his colleagues do not perform well enough. When he asks himself when this feeling of inadequacy started, he realizes it was when his father constantly criticized him for not being athletic enough. Ron never felt good enough in his father's eyes. This belief has stayed with him into adulthood. To heal, he needs to allow himself to feel inadequate and understand that it has nothing to do with his self-worth. He can acknowledge his father's criticism as harmful to him as a child, but it doesn't define him anymore. By accepting himself as he is, Ron can stop comparing himself to others and find peace within himself.

A trigger is often an indication that we are stuck in our lower self. This is why practicing self-acceptance is so important. This can cause us to react in the same way we did in our childhood, even if the situation is not the same.

Compassion meditation

By practicing self-acceptance, we can begin to understand and acknowledge our own insecurities and unaccepted traits, which will help us to stop projecting them onto others. This can lead to greater self-awareness and the ability to respond to triggers in a more mindful and intentional way. Instead of being controlled by our emotions and past experiences, we can choose to react from a place of understanding and compassion, both for ourselves and for others.

A compassion meditation can take many forms, but at its core, it involves focusing on feelings of empathy and understanding toward yourself and others.

Here is one example of how a compassion meditation might look like:

Find a quiet, comfortable place to sit where you won't be disturbed.

Begin by taking a few deep breaths and calming your mind.

Focus your attention on your breath.

Think about a person, including yourself, who is experiencing pain, suffering, or hardship. Visualize this person in your mind, and imagine their struggle and emotions.

As you visualize this person, repeat the following phrases to yourself: "May you be safe. May you be happy. May you be healthy. May you live with ease."

Next, imagine sending a warm, comforting energy to the person you are visualizing. See it enveloping them and easing their pain.

Repeat the phrases and visualizations for other people in your life, including those who are close to you and those who are distant or difficult to love.

Finally, bring your focus back to yourself. Repeat the phrases and visualizations for yourself, accepting and loving yourself just as you are.

When you're ready, gently open your eyes and bring your meditation to a close. Take a moment to reflect on how you feel now.

You may modify this practice to suit your own needs and preferences, and there are many other variations available.

Oneness—the opposite from separation.

Every time you become aware that you are bothered by someone's unlovable aspect, such as "Jake is selfish," try to think "Jake and I are selfish" instead of separating yourself from Jake and the feeling. See if you can accept this with both yourself and him. Sit with it and go as deep you can to understand more layers to it. You can also, on the other side, create a boundary around selfish people. You can avoid them, or hold distance to them. Make sure you do this from your higher self. Through understanding and love rather than from judgment.

S.⁴

Self-Esteem

Backdrop meditation: How to transform the void.

Step 1: Insight. Discover your methods of gaining love.

Finding ways to receive love starts with gaining insight into how you want to be perceived by others. To begin this process, take some time to reflect on what qualities or traits you would like others to appreciate about you. Write down three of these qualities.

Here are some examples of qualities or traits someone might write down:

- Compassionate
- Aware
- Intelligent
- Confident
- Generous
- Creative
- Honest
- Independent
- Reliable

Next, consider how it would feel if others perceived the opposite of these qualities in you. This exercise can help you understand the impact of how we present ourselves to others.

Step 2: Healing. How to transform the void.

Close your eyes and try to connect with how you're feeling in your body right now, especially around your heart, where many emotions are stored. Think about one of the three qualities you chose in the previous exercise, for example: "I want others to perceive me as smart." Consider how important it is for you to be perceived as smart, and everything you do to appear smart. This is your indirect method of getting love.

Now, try to imagine the opposite; being perceived as dumb. Imagine others around you seeing you as unaware and uneducated. Stay in that feeling for a moment. Allow it to be there within you. This is the feeling you've created behaviors around to avoid feeling. Try saying to yourself: "It's okay for me to be dumb." This means giving yourself acceptance to be imperfect. Ultimately, we want to give equal power to both dumb and smart: one is a form of escape (you're escaping from being perceived as dumb), and the other is a need (you need to be perceived as smart). Both come from programming truths created in early childhood. We want to practice accepting both sides. Allowing yourself to be seen as dumb, but also, on a deeper level, understanding that you are not. And ultimately none of these labels matter or define you.

When we don't trust our own competence, in this case feeling smart, we need external validation to feel it. This is why we need to practice integrating a feeling while also practicing letting go of the need or escape from the feeling. In this meditation, you imagine and take in the idea of being dumb for long enough that it loses its value. Of course, this doesn't mean you should start perceiving yourself as dumb, but rather removing the fear of being perceived as dumb and the control over being perceived as smart.

The second part of this meditation is telling yourself that you are smart. To avoid falling into an ego boost, you need to feel how it would feel to feel smart without having to prove it, in other words, a more grounded feeling. For example, using the affirmation: "I am smart." Feel how it feels to fully trust yourself. Sit with this until you have fully accepted, embraced, and embodied the feeling.

Meditation outlined

Connect with how you're feeling around your heart.
Think about a quality you want to be perceived as.
Imagine the opposite and allow yourself to feel it.
Say "It's okay to be imperfect" and practice accepting these sides.
Feel it and sit with it, until it loses its value or power over you.
Tell yourself "I have this quality" (the opposite feeling).
Sit with the feeling of having the quality until you fully accept it.

Examples:

Imagine you value kindness. You strive to be a kind person and often go out of your way to help others. This is your indirect way of seeking love. But now, imagine the opposite. Imagine being perceived as cruel and insensitive to others. Allow yourself to feel the discomfort and anxiety that comes with this thought. It's important to recognize that both the desire to be kind and the fear of being perceived as cruel stem from programmed beliefs created in childhood.

Imagine you value independence. You take pride in being self-sufficient and not relying on others for help. But now, imagine being perceived as distant and unapproachable. Feel the emotions that come with this thought, and remind yourself that it's okay to be perceived this way. We often strive for independence as a way of avoiding vulnerability and the fear of rejection. But in order to fully embrace and trust ourselves, we must also be able to accept our vulnerability.

Imagine you value creativity. You put a lot of effort into being original and imaginative. But now, imagine being perceived as uncreative and lacking imagination and ordinary. Allow yourself to feel the disappointment and frustration that come with this thought. Our need for being extraordinary often stems from a desire for recognition and validation. But true self-expression comes from within and does not depend on external validation.

By meditating on both sides (extremes) of the spectrum, we can learn to accept and integrate both aspects of ourselves. And ultimately be in the middle.

S.⁵

Self-Power

Backdrop meditation: How to transform your patterns.

Step 1: Insight. Discover your patterns.

Reflect on your past love relationships.

What attracted you to your partners? Identify common traits.

What caused you pain and insecurity? Identify common traits.

For example, let's consider Helena's relationships. When she meets Jack, he overwhelms her with love. He shows her that he's willing to do anything for her. He professes his love through gifts, future plans, grand gestures, and sacrifices. Helena is swept off her feet because she never came first when she was a child. The fact that Jack has a child and leaves his wife for Helena is initially a declaration of love, but it ends in jealousy, envy, and feeling left out for Helena.

A few years later, when Helena meets Henry, she's again overwhelmed by love. He tells her they are soulmates on their first date, and Helena is on cloud nine. The fact that Henry has a teenager and an ex-wife is sensitive for Helena, but she's convinced his love is strong enough to make her feel secure. When conflicts arise between Helena and the teenager, Henry sides with his son and Helena is once again left out.

Finally, Helena meets Matt and makes it clear that she won't date someone with children. Matt doesn't have any children, but he has a thriving career. However, as the passion fades, Helena is left feeling neglected and alone as Matt prioritizes his career over her.

This is Helena's pattern:

She's attracted to men who make her feel special and chosen.

She's hurt and insecure when men don't prioritize her.

If we delve deeper into Helena's history and life, we see that her father never prioritized her; he might not have even been present. The consequence is that Helena is now attracted to men who make her feel valued, but she manifests her father in the form of a boyfriend. This is her pattern.

Step 2: Healing. How to transform your patterns.

Think back to your previous relationships and what hurt you, such as feeling excluded. Reflect on a time when you felt left out and how that felt. Tell yourself, "I fully accept this feeling and allow myself to feel it."

Close your eyes and think of the first time you encountered this behavior. Often, this is between the ages of 3–8 years old. Try to gather as much information about the memory as possible. Again, imagine yourself as an adult, walking into the memory, to the child who is scared, abandoned, and hurt. Sit next to them, perhaps holding their hand or giving them a hug, showing empathy for their feelings. Stay in this feeling. The goal here is to transform the wound into self-compassion. To embody the feeling, you need to visualize it and use your imagination. For some, self-compassion is foreign and difficult to grasp, so give yourself patience and acceptance in being where you are, letting it fall into place bit by bit.

Mediation outlined

Close your eyes and take a few deep breaths. As you exhale, release any tension or stress you may be holding in your body.

Think back on your past relationships and reflect on instances where you felt hurt, such as feeling excluded. Recall the specific situation and how it felt to be left out.

Say to yourself, "I fully accept this feeling and allow myself to fully feel it."

Imagine yourself as a child, between the ages of 3–8 years old. Try to remember the first time you experienced this feeling of being blamed or not good enough.

Visualize yourself as an adult entering this memory, reaching out to the child who is scared, hurt, and alone. Show them compassion by offering them a hug or holding their hand.

Focus on the feeling of self-compassion. It may be unfamiliar and difficult at first, but be patient with yourself and allow it to come to you bit by bit.

Sit with this feeling for a few minutes, allowing it to permeate through your body and mind. The goal is to transform the hurt into self-compassion.

When you're ready, slowly open your eyes and take a deep breath, feeling more connected to your inner child and empowered with self-compassion. Remember, the process of transforming hurt into self-compassion takes time and practice. Be kind to yourself.

Example:

Imagine you are Tim, and you're reflecting on your past relationships. You realize that a pattern has emerged—you constantly feel judged and like you're never good enough in your relationships. No matter how hard you try, you feel like nothing you do is ever enough.

You remember how this pattern started, and you trace it back to your childhood. You recall how your mother constantly criticized and judged you, never seeming to be satisfied with anything you did. This has left you feeling inadequate and like you'll never be good enough, no matter what you do.

You've fallen in love with the opposite of your mother, someone who praises you and gives you a lot of validation and compliments. This person makes you feel good about yourself and helps you avoid the negative feelings of inadequacy that your mother instilled in you.

However, despite the initial rush of validation and praise, you soon realize that this person also disappoints you. They may not be able to live up to the idealized image you have in your head, and eventually, you're faced with the same feelings of judgment and not being good enough.

This cycle continues to repeat, and you're stuck in this pattern of attracting people who validate you, but end up disappointing or criticizing you.

Now, imagine that you are going back in time to when you were a child, to the time when your mother's criticism and judgment first started affecting you. You visualize yourself as an adult, walking into that memory and sitting next to your younger self, comforting and consoling the child who feels scared, hurt, and judged. You show them love and understanding, and as you do this, you begin to feel self-compassion. Feel the wound with compassion. Take a moment to sit with this feeling. See if you can embody this feeling and really feel it in your body. If it's difficult to feel at first, that's okay. Just be patient and give yourself time to let it settle in.

By connecting with your inner child and showing them love and understanding, you begin to heal the wounds from your past and break the cycle of attracting people who judge you. You see more clearly and you are perhaps no longer judging yourself. You start to realize that you are enough, just as you are, and that you don't need external validation to feel good about yourself.

The pendulum between two extremes

When old patterns arise, they may express themselves in a trigger, such as frustration over something. Observe your reaction patterns and try to apply the opposite: do the opposite. This is a good way to move from a behavior that has become destructive to a new temporary approach. The goal is to arrive at harmony between two extremes.

Example: Helena is irritated because Matt doesn't respond when she texts him. Hours go by and she gets no response. She probably feels consciously or unconsciously deprioritized. Her wounds are activated. However, it doesn't have to be true that she is deprioritized, but it feels true for Helena at this moment. Helena's defense mechanism for being deprioritized is to calibrate her emotions with friends, punish her boyfriend by not responding when he finally texts her, or plan to end the relationship.

Instead, Helena should close her eyes, feel, and maybe silently tell herself that it's okay for her to feel this way, but that she doesn't have to feel this way. Because nobody has deprioritized her, and even if she feels deprioritized, it's okay. Helena prioritizes Helena, and that is the only prioritization that is important right now. Helena needs her boyfriend to feel valuable, but by practicing not needing him at all, she moves from one extreme to another. And that's okay during a transition period, but over a longer period, the new behavior can become just as destructive. To reach a harmony between two extremes, she can tell herself that her boyfriend is probably doing his best, he's not perfect, and that's okay. She doesn't need him to feel valuable, but at the same time it's just as okay to need him. She might also state this to him in her vulnerability: "I am struggling with feeling secure when I feel unprioritized."

Helena is pathologically avoiding the feeling of worthlessness. If she instead gets curious about the feeling of worthlessness, which often expresses itself in frustration (fear), through healing and integration, the feeling will over time have less power over her. She will be okay with being in the feeling and therefore not have to avoid it (bypass it) by calibrating with friends, revenge, or ending it. Helena can also do the opposite in her choice of partner. Notice if she attracts unavailable men, and then, early on choose to not engage further.

Another example: John is someone who often feels anxious in social situations. He feels uncomfortable in large groups and often avoids social events. He judges himself for being unsocial. When he experiences this internal or maybe even external judgment, he may feel the urge to withdraw. However, he can tell himself that it's okay to feel nervous in social situations. He can come to terms that he is an introvert and sensitive, and that he doesn't like to be around too many people at the same time. By accepting, embracing, and honoring his feelings, John can be more confident about who he is. Also, as humans, we have an innate need for connection and belonging. Being part of a community can provide us with a sense of purpose, belonging, and support. However, it's also important to recognize that not all relationships are healthy or beneficial for us. It's essential to be mindful of the dynamics at play in our relationships and to evaluate whether they are contributing to our overall well-being and growth.

By cultivating healthy relationships and connections, we can foster a sense of community and belonging while also prioritizing our own well-being and growth. It's a delicate balance, but by being aware of our own needs and boundaries, we can form meaningful connections with others while also taking care of ourselves.

S.⁶

Self-Worth

Backdrop meditation: How to transform your survival strategies.

Step 1: Insight. Discover your survival strategies.

What is your primary survival strategy?

Circle one of your most frequently used strategies. Be as honest and truthful as you can.

Fight: Argue and defend yourself and assert your boundaries

For example:

Outburst in anger—Screaming, hitting, violence.
Self-harm behavior—Engaging in behavior that intentionally harms yourself.
Melodramatic—Overreacting or exaggerating emotions or situations.

Flight: Avoiding

For example:

Bypassing—Denying a problem or issue.
Explanation—Explaining away a problem or issue to minimize its impact or avoid dealing with it.
Projection—Attributing your own negative qualities or feelings onto another person or thing.
Humor—Using humor to deflect.
Intellectualization—Rational explanations to avoid or distance yourself from emotions.
Beautification—Seeing something as more positive or beautiful than it actually is.

Freeze: Struggle to come up with a response

For example:

Shut down—Day sleep, resting, scrolling.

Dissociate—Not engaging in any feelings.
Isolate—Withdrawing emotionally or physically.

Fawn: Avoiding conflict

For example:

Repression—Ignoring unwanted thoughts or feelings.
People please—Goes out of your way to do things for others.
Apologizes excessively—Avoid upsetting the other person and maintain a positive relationship.
Taking on guilt—Assuming responsibility or blame for something that is not your fault.

Step 2: Healing. How to transform your survival strategies.
Reflect on a current situation where you have used the strategy that you have identified. Ask yourself, when was the first time I came into contact with this strategy, and when was the first time I needed to use it. It's completely okay to use your intellect here and try to find a memory. If you want to go deeper, try to reach your alpha state and let your intellect ask your subconscious when the first time was.

Meditation outlined

Think of a current situation where you used the strategy that you selected.

Ask yourself: "When was the first time I encountered this strategy, the first time I needed it?"

Trust the process. It may come up in fragments, a feeling, or intuition.

Explore the memory through your imagination and extend it. What happened before and after? Trust your intuition.

Gain clarity and understanding of why you needed this strategy to survive. Why was it good for you? And what is the shadow side? Why is it bad for you?

Examples:

At the age of eighteen, Craig felt liberated and free when he moved away from his family of origin. He needed to distance himself from them to evolve, and so flight became his survival strategy. During the three years that followed, he was in his element and people were drawn to him and his light. However, he also felt unsupported and alone. He avoided dwelling on these feelings and soldiered on.

Years later, Craig left behind a job and city that no longer suited him, and once again he felt liberated and began to explore his spiritual life. Yet, he also felt scared about how he would provide for himself, and experienced feelings of loneliness and insecurity about where he truly belonged. He reflected on all the times he had moved away from something and realized that each time he had ended a relationship he evolved. But he also felt alone and unsupported.

As Craig sat with these thoughts, he began to feel the grief of his original family and the fact that he never had parents to support him. He started to confront the wounds of his survival strategy, recognizing that it had served him well in the past, but it was now holding him back.

Sasha tends to always put herself last in her relationships. She often prioritizes the needs and wants of her partners over her own, leading to feelings of resentment and frustration and she has outbursts of anger. She uses the survival strategy fight. Sarah can remember a specific moment in her childhood when her parents constantly dismissed her feelings and needs in favor of her siblings. This left her feeling unheard and unimportant, and she learned to prioritize others in order to feel loved and accepted, but at the same time she needed to scream to be seen.

As Sasha sat with these thoughts, she began to feel anger and grief for not being heard or understood as a child. She also found herself constantly sacrificing her own desires to make her partner happy, leading to feelings of unhappiness and resentment and was easily triggered. She often found herself screaming and yelling to express herself. As she reflects more deeply, she begins to realize that her wounds are lodged deep within her throat. She notices that she experiences more frequent soreness, infections, and inflammation in this area than others. As she continues to sit with these feelings, she becomes aware of the emotional blockages and unexpressed emotions that have accumulated in her throat chakra, causing physical discomfort and pain.

With this newfound awareness, she begins to take steps to heal her throat chakra. She starts to express herself more freely and authentically, and the physical symptoms that once plagued her begin to dissipate.

Pernilla experienced the loss of her brother at a young age, and her parents coped by shutting down their emotions and never discussing it. With nowhere to turn for support or comfort, Pernilla suppressed her own grief. As the years passed, she began to feel increasingly unmotivated, tired, and unfocused. She withdrew from others and became ashamed of who she was. She felt like her emotions were "too much for others to handle."

Pernilla came to realize that she had shut down emotionally as a way of mirroring her parents' behavior. She also recognized that she had developed a resistance to her own feelings. This resistance became unconsciously something others picked up on and mirrored. Pernilla took it personally and dwelled deeper into her programming: "I'll need to shut down my emotions to belong in a group."

Years later, in a group therapy, Pernilla began to feel compassion for herself and her feelings. She allowed herself to cry for all the years of suppressed grief, and importantly, she did so in the presence of others. Through this process of emotional work, Pernilla also came to understand that her long-term back pain was connected to her lack of emotional support. In order to fully integrate this understanding, Pernilla needed to show her grief without resistance and allow others to witness her.

When we resist our own feelings, others are often inclined to mirror that resistance, which can lead us to feel abandoned and unsupported. Back pain is highly linked to lack of support. Our own and secondary others.

S.7

Self-Support

3

FEEL TO HEAL

Moving from intellectualizing emotions to feeling them can be a powerful shift. And for many, intellectualizing emotions is a deep integrated survival strategy, defense mechanism, or a coping mechanism.

Examples of how you can feel to heal:

Emotional awareness: Take the time to pay attention to your body and notice the physical sensations that accompany your emotions. For instance, if you feel jealous, you may notice a tightness in your chest or a racing heart. By first admitting to and then acknowledging these potentially shameful feelings and sensations, and then sitting with them, you can start to understand and experience your emotions more fully. This can of course be applied to a wide range of emotions, including grief, sadness, frustration, powerlessness, restlessness, and many others. By paying attention to the messages of these emotions, we can deepen our understanding of ourselves and our experiences, and ultimately develop greater emotional intelligence and resilience.

Emotional communication: Instead of simply thinking about your emotions, try to communicate with them. Ask yourself what message they have for you and where they are situated in your body. If you truly sit with this, you may reveal some deep wounds and realizations. Intellectualizing emotions can be a way to protect yourself from feeling overwhelmed or uncomfortable. However, in the long run, it can also lead to a sense of disconnection.

The terms "lower self" and "higher self" are sometimes used in reference to the subconscious and superconscious mind, respectively. The subconscious mind represents the part of ourselves that operates below our conscious awareness, including automatic behaviors, habits, and emotions that we may not fully understand or control. The superconscious mind, on the other hand, represents the highest levels of consciousness and awareness, where we can access our inner wisdom, creativity, and spiritual insight.

When we speak of distinguishing between our lower and higher selves, **we are essentially talking about the process of becoming more aware of the automatic behaviors and negative thought patterns that may be rooted in our subconscious, and learning to access the wisdom and insight of our superconscious.** By doing so, we can move beyond the limitations of our lower selves and tap into our higher selves.

Emotions

Ground emotions are the primary emotions that serve as the foundation for all other emotions. These emotions are thought to be universal and include anger, sadness, shame, guilt, joy, love, hate, and fear. These emotions are often described as raw and intense, and they serve as the building blocks for more complex emotions. Emotions play a vital role in our lives and are an important aspect of the human experience. **While emotions can sometimes be difficult to navigate, understanding their positive aspects can help us to develop a more positive and healthy. relationship with them.** Here are some of the key positive aspects of some of the most common emotions:

Anger: Passion and life force. Anger is often thought of as a negative emotion, but it can also provide a sense of passion and motivation. When harnessed correctly, anger can be a powerful force that drives us to make positive changes in our lives and fight for what we believe in.

Fear: Protection. Fear is a natural instinct that helps to protect us from danger and preserve our survival. It can motivate us to take action to avoid danger and ensure our safety. By recognizing the positive aspects of fear, we can learn to harness its power to help us stay safe and secure.

Sadness: Authenticity and vulnerability. Sadness is often associated with feelings of loss or disappointment, but it can also make us feel more authentic and vulnerable. When we allow ourselves to feel our sadness, it can help us to connect with others on a deeper level and develop greater empathy and understanding.

Shame: Pathway to self-compassion. Shame is often a difficult emotion to confront, but it can also be a pathway to self-compassion. By recognizing and acknowledging our shame, we can begin to understand our own thoughts, behaviors, and actions, and use that understanding to develop greater self-compassion and self-awareness.

Guilt: Pathway to accountability. Guilt is often associated with a sense of wrongdoing, but it can also be a pathway to accountability. By recognizing and accepting our feelings of guilt, we can take steps to make amends and become more accountable for our actions.

Hate: Disconnection. Hate is a powerful emotion that can indicate a disconnection from others and from ourselves. By understanding and recognizing the role that hate plays in our lives, we can work to build greater connection and understanding with others, and develop greater compassion and empathy.

Love: Connection. Love is one of the most powerful and transformative emotions, and it is associated with feelings of connection and bonding with others.

Joy: Joy is a light and uplifting emotion that brings playfulness and a sense of fun to our lives.

The window of tolerance

By understanding the positive aspects of our emotions, we can develop trust and acceptance towards them. However, during intense self-healing processes, it is common for a multitude of stored emotions to resurface. The "window of tolerance" is a term used in psychology and neuroscience to describe the range of emotional and physiological states that an individual can tolerate without becoming overwhelmed or dysregulated. This concept is based on the idea that every individual has a unique range of emotional arousal that they can tolerate before becoming either hyperaroused (e.g., anxious, angry, panicked) or hypoaroused (e.g., numb, disconnected, dissociated). When an individual's level of emotional arousal exceeds their window of tolerance, they may become dysregulated, which can lead to a range of symptoms including anxiety, depression, substance abuse, and trauma-related disorders. However, when an individual is able to stay within their window of tolerance, they are better able to manage stress, regulate their emotions, and maintain healthy relationships.

The window of tolerance can vary depending on a range of factors, including genetics, past experiences, and current stressors. Some individuals may have a wider window of tolerance than others, while others may have a narrower range.

For example, if someone has a history of being criticized, they may be more sensitive to feelings of shame and may experience shame more easily and intensely than others in similar situations. Similarly, if someone has experienced physical trauma, they may be more easily triggered by feelings of fear or anxiety in response to perceived threats. They are outside the window of tolerance.

When emotions are suppressed or avoided, they can become pent up and build up over time, making them more difficult to manage and control. This can lead to a heightened emotional response to even minor stressors and make it difficult to navigate daily life. It is important to understand your own window of tolerance and develop strategies to stay within this range, such as emotional work to regulate your emotions and respond effectively to stress.

Healing is all about self compassion.

Your emotions are your bread and butter. Your emotions are the lifeblood of your being. They are the source of your deepest insights, your most profound joys, and your greatest challenges. Ignoring or suppressing them is like cutting off your own nourishment and vitality. Take a moment to reflect on an emotion that you typically don't like or struggle with, such as embarrassment, boredom, restlessness, jealousy, or anger. Do you find yourself unconsciously scrolling through your phone when bored? Do you berate yourself for feeling angry? How do you treat yourself when you're scared about your financial situation? Maybe you feel that someone else's success or happiness means that you are lacking in some way. Instead of avoiding or suppressing these emotions, try sitting with them. Take a few deep breaths and allow yourself to fully experience the emotion. See if you can identify any underlying messages or insights that it may be offering you. **Your emotions are like your inner compass, guiding you toward your deepest truths and desires. When you learn to listen to them and honor them, you open yourself up to compassion.**

S.⁸

Self-Love

Higher self meditation

Close your eyes and imagine you are a luxurious bed and breakfast, a haven for holistic spirituality. You are an exceptional host, radiating warmth and kindness, with an inclusive and open-minded approach. Your guests are your emotions, coming and going as they please, seeking refuge in your serene abode. You are in your higher self.

As the loving host, you are not attached to any particular emotion, allowing them to arrive and depart with ease. Your guests feel safe and welcomed in your hotel, thriving under your attentive care. Although, at times, cleaning up after them may not always be a pleasant task, you do so with grace and understanding.

Now, imagine if you were not a good host, if you forced your emotions to stay and excluded some of them, treating them like outcasts. Your once peaceful retreat would become a toxic environment, where some guests would feel trapped and others would feel unwelcome. Your guests see it as a prison and are full of resistance when they visit. Some of them, or actually all of them, don't want to visit, but they have no other home. As the host for this prison, you try to get rid of your guest by forcing them on to someone else's hotel. For example, you try to give shame away and keep love. This makes it uncomfortable for love so love doesn't want to stay either, or at least SHE doesn't feel safe. Yes, you are in your lower self.

Now, imagine that your bed and breakfast is the world and you are the host of an enormous retreat. How do you want people to feel in your world? Welcome, free, and safe, or unwelcomed, controlled, and dismissed? The choice is yours, and the power is in your hands to create a world where everyone is accepted and embraced, just like in a peaceful, loving retreat.

S.9

Self-Confidence

Thank you, Emotions

I greet you with love and gratitude. I cherish each and every one of you, and I embrace the role you play in my life. I understand that you are not always easy to handle, but I am here to listen and to offer comfort.

You are a welcome presence in my life, and I will never turn you away. I recognize the power you hold, and I embrace your strength with open arms. I understand that some may struggle with you, but I invite them to take the time to get to know you. I see you in others, and I feel you with empathy and compassion. I believe that we can all benefit from a deeper understanding of you, and I invite those who may be struggling to find safety in your embrace. Together, let us continue on this journey, exploring and learning from each other. I love you, Emotions, and I am here to support you in all that you do.

Thank you.

Thank you, Mom and Dad

I want to express my deepest gratitude and love for the two of you. Despite your imperfections, I see you both as perfect in your own unique ways. Your love brought me into this world, and for that, I am forever thankful.

You set me on a journey of self-discovery, a journey that has allowed me to delve into the depths of my soul and truly understand who I am. Through the ups and downs, I have learned to embrace my experiences and find beauty in even the darkest moments. I understand that you never intended to cause harm, and I have forgiven both of you and myself for any pain we may have caused each other.

The person I am today is a result of everything I have experienced, the good and the bad, and I wouldn't have it any other way. The journey you both unconsciously set me on has allowed me to become compassionate to myself, and for that, I am eternally grateful.

Mom and Dad, I want you to know that you hold a special place in my heart. I love you both deeply, I will either hold on to you or let you go. I will cherish the impact you have had on my life.

With respect, frustration, anger, disappointment, love, and gratitude, Thank You.

Thank you, Inner Child

Hi little you.

It's been a journey for us both, hasn't it? In the past, I tried to ignore your presence, to push you away, and to start anew. But you kept coming back, reminding me of who I was and what I've been through.

Now, I see you.

I see you as a guide, a friend, and my greatest source of love. I am grateful for the opportunity to learn how to parent and care for you. You are my top priority, my greatest love. You bring light, joy, and happiness into my life, but also sadness, shame, guilt, fear, passion, and anger. You embody everything that makes me who I am, and I embrace it all.

I promise to always be there for you, to hold your hand and support you through the good times and the bad. I will never abandon you again, for you are me. My light. My force. My energy.

Thank you.

Thank you, Reader

First, I want to express my sincere gratitude to you for taking the time to read this book, a project I created with my dear client Ninni. She wrote the first part with a lot of self-distance and bravery. We both wrote the book for ourselves, to learn and grow, but also for you. I hope you found something meaningful within these pages that resonates with your soul. It certainly moved mine in so many ways. I am Ninni, as well as Karin and all the other people in this book. If not in this life, then in another. I can relate to it all with unconditional love.

I also want to take a moment to emphasize my deep love for you. Yes, you! It may sound cheesy, but it's true. I believe that we are all interconnected, and our paths have crossed for a reason.

I know firsthand that this journey can be challenging and overwhelming at times, but I want you to know that I am here with you. I may not be physically present, but I am sending you love, support, and encouragement every step of the way. And if I may be so bold, I would love to meet you someday, whether online or at my retreat center. You and all your different parts are invited.

So, dear Reader, I hope this book has provided you with tools, comfort, inspiration, and humor along the way. Let us remember to be kind to ourselves and each other, always approaching this earth school journey with compassion and awareness. It's as ongoing as life itself, and there will be setbacks, disappointments, and new wounds along the way. But that is all as it should be, a natural part of the process called life. With every setback comes a new revelation, learning, and understanding. Just stick with it, with love—I sure will do my best.

With all my love and care,

April